Friendship and Healing

Friendship and Healing

THE DREAMS OF JOHN ADAMS AND BENJAMIN RUSH

Sheila Dickman Zarrow

CHIRON PUBLICATIONS · WILMETTE, ILLINOIS

Book and cover design by Imaginary Office.
Printed in the United States of America.

Library of Congress Cataloging-in-Publication Data

Zarrow, Sheila Dickman, 1952-
  Friendship and healing : the dreams of John Adams and Benjamin Rush / Sheila Dickman Zarrow.
    p. cm.
  Includes bibliographical references and index.
  ISBN 978-1-888602-50-0 (trade pbk. : alk. paper)
  1. Adams, John, 1735-1826--Psychology. 2. Adams, John, 1735-1826--Friends and associates. 3. Adams, John, 1735-1826--Correspondence. 4. Rush, Benjamin, 1746-1813--Psychology. 5. Rush, Benjamin, 1746-1813--Friends and associates. 6. Rush, Benjamin, 1746-1813--Correspondence. I. Title.

  E302.Z37 2010
  973.4'4092--dc22

                         2010022284

My dear Friend Rush,
If I could dream as much wit as you, I think I should wish to go
to sleep for the rest of my life, retaining, however, [someone] to
awake me once in 24 hours to dinner...."

—*Letters,* John Adams to Benjamin Rush, 4 March 1809

[Dreaming is] as much a native faculty as memory or
imagination.... [It is] a source of knowledge, so necessary to
individual comfort and social existence [that] has not been made
dependent upon our senses, nor left to the slow inductions of
reason.... this faculty has not yet found its way into our systems
of physiology.

—Benjamin Rush, M.D., *Medical Inquiries and Observations,* 1812

contents

ix   List of Figures

xi   Preface

1   CHAPTER ONE
Going Home

15   CHAPTER TWO
John Adams at Home

23   CHAPTER THREE
Rush's Dream of Mercury

43   CHAPTER FOUR
Adams's "Annimatical" Dream

53   CHAPTER FIVE
Rush's Poem "After a Night of Perplexing Dreams"

69   CHAPTER SIX
Benjamin Rush's Prophetic Dream

75   CHAPTER SEVEN
John Adams's Theater Dream: A Play Within a Dream

87   CHAPTER EIGHT
Hobby/Chiron

91   CHAPTER NINE
Thomas Jefferson

95   Epilogue

99   Postscript

103   Endnotes

109   Bibliography

111   Acknowledgments

112   Index

figures

1. *Gabriel Weather Vane (Technique)*, Lucielle Chabot

2. *John Adams*, Gilbert Stuart

3. *Benjamin Rush*, Charles Willson Peale

4. John Adams's home in Quincy, Massachusetts

5. *Christ Church, after van Gogh's* Starry Night, Jennifer Leigh Erickson

6. *Mercury/Hermes*, Giovanni da Bologna

7. *Mercury with cock and goat*, Artus Quellinus

8. *History of Medicine*, Conrad A. Albrizio

9. *Captain Isaac Hull, USN*

10. *Captain Jacob Jones, USN*

11. *The Capture of the* Frolic

12. *Sarah Siddons as "Tragic Muse,"* Francis Haward

13. *Sarah Siddons*, Sir William Beechey

14. *Chiron*, Carrie Judem

15. *Thomas Jefferson*, Gilbert Stuart

16. *Gabriel Weather Vane*, Lucielle Chabot

Color gallery follows p. 52.

I am grateful to David McCullough, whose brilliant book on John Adams was so comfortable and familiar to me that I felt Adams's living presence awaken and look around, as if to see how we are doing with his extraordinary experiment. This same effect spread across the country as the book became a best seller. Adams's popularity, which he would have thoroughly enjoyed had it come during his lifetime, struck a chord among readers of history and raised an interest in history among the general American public. It seemed to me that the emotional sense of pride I felt when reading the book was felt by many others who were touched by the beauty and affection with which McCullough wrote about Adams.

In his Jefferson Lecture, delivered in May 2003, McCullough quoted Edith Hamilton, an historian writing when the architect of analytical psychology, Carl Gustav Jung, was young. She wrote:

> what a refuge and strength the past can be to us in the troubled
> present. Religion can be a stronghold for the untroubled vision
> of the eternal, but there are others too. We have many silent
> sanctuaries in which we can find breathing space to free ourselves
> from the personal—to rise above our harassed and perplexed
> minds and catch sight of values that are stable which no selfish and
> timorous preoccupations can make waver because they are the hard
> won, permanent possessions of humanity. When the world is storm
> driven and the bad that happens and the worst that threatens are
> so urgent as to shut out everything else from view—then we need
> to know all the strong fortresses of the spirit which men have built
> throughout the ages.[1]

This was quite true, up to a point. But the age of reason was nearly past and the age of psychology would soon bring to light a whole new resource that men had not built—one that was inherent in human nature. Among the ways we come to know about these influences on human thought and behavior is through the visual language and symbolic expression of dreams. Dreams have meaning well beyond the personal and the present. They have qualities, roots, and tendrils that stretch throughout the unseen, unknown, inner world of our psyches. There, while we sleep, they make connections between our own lives and those of others throughout history, mythology, and the eternal in all its forms.

I developed a great friendship and mutual understanding with Adams when I was a teenager skipping school most Fridays, sitting at the foot of his woefully inadequate statue. It was not far from—and certainly unjustly not in the center of—downtown Worcester, Massachusetts, where he used to teach before he was president—and where I was avoiding school two hundred years later. The statue was a miserable and demeaning tribute, and I felt it hurt his feelings very much. He was therapist and inspiration to me. He was perhaps a little bit Freudian inasmuch as he did not say much during our sessions. But he was a good listener. And I listened too, in that way that the psyche has for hearing the unspoken. We both had a lot to think about. I had a cloak of limitations to which I had become accustomed when I was younger, but which now no longer fit. Adams had been through it, too. He lost his equivocal mantle of power when he lost reelection. He had had to find his way to discover and live a new definition of himself for the latter part of his lifetime. But by the time I met John Adams he was a changed man from how you may have heard or read about him. There he was, standing, not much larger than life size, on a worn cement block. We were also off center on the grass in the middle of the street, and the traffic circle went around and off in so many directions that no intelligent driver could really take an eye off the road to get a good look and remember him or what he meant to them. (Meanwhile not many people remember anything about Dr. Benjamin Rush.)

If you take a figure like Adams from the past, now transformed a thousand times from his life through his death and on into a constellation and then a cosmos of histories, hundreds and thousands of transformational processes, the alchemical outcome you will find is a mythic, living symbol. When I sat with him, the statue itself felt alive with movement as if motes of influence from every era were living things that had come forward through time to hear and adhere to the myth of his being. Adams was typically valiant about the not-much-more-than-life-size statue. Perhaps it is just as well he had not seen it. There was hardly enough room for me to sit at his feet, but it was there on its plinth, where we met for three years, that I found beauty in the silent sanctuaries of the mind.

My study of Benjamin Rush was not my fault. I was writing along, analyzing Adams's dreams, faithful to his life and times and, as well as I was able, to the symbolic and archetypal overarching influences reflected in them—when I found Rush's dreams in his letters to Adams. I began to read his books and the histories. Then I went to Pennsylvania and read letters and poems written in his own hand, in the first person, in his living present. There followed three years during which I sat at the base of Rush's indistinct image with my mind soaking up impressions of him from the pages he wrote and the pages written about him.

Then I had a dream. In my dream I had begun, tentatively and with great insecurities, to integrate Rush's story and dreams into my book. I started to pour myself some wine, and it would have spilled and ruined the keyboard had Rush not stepped into my writing room and held a fine long-stemmed, etched, antique wineglass under the pouring wine, catching and containing it. Having been visited by this elegant spirit, I was, and remain, concerned about my human clumsiness in conveying the symbolic, fragile container with the essence of its distilled contents through the ages to you. I have been careful. It took time, and I think Adams became impatient about it, because it was not long before he came to the door of my writing room in a dream.

He was in 1809, and I in 2009. He was dressed in his usual gray-brown way. Or maybe the suit had been darker, maybe his black suit. But the whole fabric of his appearance as I saw it bespoke an argument between his eminent Revolutionary presence, and its opposite, a certain custom-made simplicity. Retired now, he thought of himself as former-president-farmer John. I was happy to see Adams. He really is an old friend. He just came in and leaned against the threshold of my writing room doorway, arms akimbo, hat dangling from his hand. He gave me "the look" and tapped his foot impatiently. I looked up and nodded too. When I awoke, I felt great pressure to write—for him.

What followed was a series of rapid, disorderly, intuitive emanations from my bewildered mind. As an inner figure Adams had never really asked me for anything before—and I had only recently come to know Dr. Rush. What should I write? Wasn't I already working at it? Was there a particular letter I should attend to? Which of the dreams? What does my animus want? It took the entire unfolding of the story and their dreams before I began to recognize the paradox of how Adams and Rush lived with me during my lifetime, and why I must write about them—for myself. As I neared completion of this book, the answer came in a pretty dream of mine that delivered its sense-making conclusion. I will share it with you when we get there.

SHEILA DICKMAN ZARROW, PH.D.

CALIFORNIA 2010

FIG. 1 *Gabriel Weather Vane (Technique)* (1939) by Lucielle Chabot. National Gallery of Art, Washington, D.C.

Going Home

JOHN ADAMS
Washington, D.C., 4 March 1801, 3:30 a.m.

The public coach ran more or less on time, depending on the weather and conditions along the unpaved roads. Its scheduled stop outside the White House was at 4 a.m. To get down there on time, John Adams, his nephew Billy Shaw, and his servant John Briesler had some hauling to do around 3:30 a.m. Adams was clearing out four years' worth of stuff. Not that he wanted to leave—but having lost his bid for reelection he was going home.

It was his habit since long before his White House days to keep a running record of events in notebooks and diaries, on random loose pages, on any handy scraps of paper. He saved both drafts and finished forms, thinking he might organize them all during his retirement. To this massive collection was added four years' worth of papers written while he was president. Among his precious pages are the original four sheets on which he had made his own copy of Jefferson's draft of the Declaration of Independence. Many of the papers had been sent home during the course of his time in Washington. His wife Abigail had gone ahead, taking most of their personal belongings and much of the remaining written material with her.

The Adamses' home was a comfortable, unpainted colonial-style house in Braintree, Massachusetts. There was little space in it to sort out or store the homecoming collection. Not surprisingly, the time came when Adams wrote in a letter to Louisa Catherine Adams that "the House [needs to be] put in a little order, which is covered with trunks, Books and papers, not confined to my sleeping room and the parlour, but every chamber in the House. For instance, in your uncles room, ranged in two rows, lie—I will get up and count them—no less than Eighteen large packages..." still not unpacked since the White House days.[2] Eventually Adams would turn the task of organizing it all over to his son John Quincy Adams, with the note, "I shall leave you an inheritance sufficiently tormenting, for example, The huge Pile of family Letters, will make you Alternately laugh and cry, fret and fume, stamp and scold as they do me."[3] Later, John Quincy Adams built the stone library next door to the Old House especially to protect the papers from fire.[4] But John Quincy, increasingly immersed in his own political life and continuing his father's predilection for writing and collecting papers, in short order doubled the stack of work to be done. At this point, John Quincy turned the project of putting his own papers, and his father's, in order over to his son Charles.[5]

For the time being, upon leaving the White House, Adams, Shaw, and Briesler were loaded down with whatever remaining stacks of clutter they could handle.

Bundled up against the cold and ready to go, John Adams would have taken one last look around the house he was so proud to have occupied. He was pleased with how he and Abigail had fitted the place out. It was comfortable and elegant. He took particular pleasure in the fact that it did not look like a king's palace. It was a residence embodying the ruling principles for which it stood. A symbol of authority articulated in Americana. Here and there on walls and tables of the near-empty rooms America's memorabilia recounted the historic journey out of the kingdom and into democracy. Some of the items were more personal to him than others. They memorialized his own participation and recalled half a lifetime of ideals, work, determination, accomplishments. A copy of the completed Declaration of Independence, now twenty-five years old, hung on the wall. Adams was forty, and his friend Benjamin Rush only thirty, when they had signed the original.

He remembered the tension while waiting days, and sometimes weeks, for the riders to arrive, one from each of the sixteen colonial states—each having decided whether to sign the Declaration—knowing full well that it would result in a revolutionary war. The arrival of each one delivering their consent raised the stakes, but the undeclared war had already turned the landscape of everyday life into battlefields. The names of towns attacked by the British to suppress the rebellion prior to the Declaration had already become monuments in the collective psyche of America—Concord, Lexington, Breeds Hill, Bunker Hill. Gravestones followed the field hospitals as though they were building a road to heaven.

As in most great mythic stories, when the king is out of order, the people in the kingdom suffer the bad weather of his distress. Colonial submission to the empire of King George III had long since slumped into an empire of habit. But as the weather of his rule darkened, that binding, borrowed garment became increasingly uncomfortable in America's climate. The people sought to mediate it. Then they sought to throw it off. Soon all things borne across the ocean from Britain carried the stigma of a king turned against his subjects. The arrival of a shipment of highly taxed tea from Britain tipped the alterity principle into action.[6] The Boston Tea Party was just such an alteration. Tossing the tea into Boston Harbor broke the habit of conformity—and awareness of new possibilities came into existence. The waters of the harbor steeped like a symbolic gestation all through the shapeless Revolution. Its effect was absorbed into the psyche of the colonists, and what they called themselves changed as though they had wrestled with an angel; "colonists" became "patriots" and "citizens." The harbor, like a womb, set itself in firm opposition to the intrusion of foreign objects while the new awareness of its own authority and potential was generating. When the fleet returned and anchored in and around the bay and Boston Harbor, they were unaware that they rode upon an activated living symbol.

America's greatest military weakness was that it had a long coastline and no navy. British ships seemed invulnerable until Henry Knox, yet another fabulous nearly forgotten Revolutionary figure, rescued fifty-one abandoned British cannons and assorted artillery from a battlefield, dragged them undetected all the way from New York, and with his men set them up under cover of night at Dorchester Heights—with a good view and within cannon range of the harbor. The surprise barrage came from on high, right into the ships in the American "teacup," and the British fleet high-tailed it out of Boston Harbor—apparently toward New York.

All the states had voted to sign the Declaration except New York. Intelligence had it that the British fleet that fled Boston Harbor was now heading there. Under attack by the British and their German mercenaries even as the signing was taking place, New York may have hedged its bet and not signed in part because things did not look too promising from where they stood.

The official Declaration of War followed directly upon the signing of the Declaration of Independence.

The beautiful handwritten copy of the Declaration is now a protected national treasure, but Adams's copy of the draft, and his copy of the completed work, along with some of the scraps, scratches, and notes, were jammed into his baggage to take home. Other odds and ends of papers and drafts of ideas for the Constitution and a new form of government were in among the crates. Some were taken home, some were left behind. Many are, to this day, still unceremoniously stored in crates and boxes in Philadelphia, Boston, and Washington, D.C. His old friend

Dr. Benjamin Rush would suggest years later, when Adams was feeling bad because he missed the creativity and excitement of those times, that he write about his life. Adams responded he would not. "To rummage trunks, letter books, bits of journals, and great heaps of bundles of old papers is a dreadful bondage…" Eventually their correspondence itself became an outlet for creative expression and was healing for both Adams and Rush.

Adams looked across the room to the wall with images of Washington's inauguration—practically yesterday, twelve years ago. Washington was offered, but did not want, a third term. He told Adams he was happy to be going home, and that he thought he would be happier at home than Adams would be being president. Adams longed to go home. But he did not envision happiness for his future yet—except in small ways. The image of wholeness for his presidency, as it had formed in his mind's eye, included the next four years. The ideas that he planned to enact following his reelection were no less crucial to him for the security of the nation than were his earlier ideas for the formation of the nation in the first place. For example, he was particularly determined that ships be built and a navy trained because the country was most vulnerable to attack by way of the ocean and rivers. Losing his forum was like falling off a cliff. Adams felt lost in the world he had helped to create.

In the leaving of the White House, Adams was also leaving his natural, best way of being—that is, as a thinking man with innate leadership ability, exercising his power to take action. Not having been reelected dropped him into his least practiced way of being. The impotent political condition imposed redirection of his energies inward, toward introversion and introspection, in place of extraversion and action. This alteration would become increasingly distressing for Adams. Ever a warm and loving man with his family, and always a brilliant, sharp, and active man in the community, he was nevertheless new and inexperienced, and not very

FIG. 2 *John Adams* by Gilbert Stuart. National Gallery of Art, Washington, D.C.
FIG. 3 *Benjamin Rush*, portrait by Charles Wilson Peale after painting by
Thomas Sully. National Historical Park, Philadelphia.

good at and not very happy about this turn toward the unfamiliar
inner world.

No one had ever not been reelected before. It was a disaster for
Adams. Even his election four years earlier had been tinged with
disappointment. Back then most Americans wanted Washington
to stay for a third term. Washington declined, and Adams felt the
slump in their spirit when he was sworn in essentially as the people's second choice. Then there was Jefferson. The way the system
worked at the time was that whoever came in second in the election became vice president. The vote was close—but Adams and
Jefferson were not. It had been the vision of the founders that
following an election the relationship of the political adversaries
would morph into something of a bipartisan team. But the imperfection of this idea became clear on its very first trial. As often
as not, while Adams was president, Jefferson was working against
him behind the scenes.

Nevertheless, Adams was happy to be president and galvanized the same level of focused, purposeful determination in exercising his presidency that he generated in support of his Herculean efforts during the Revolution.

Voted out, he stuffed the remainder of his giant reservoir of internal resources back into himself to take home.

Adams was in a hurry now. He wanted to leave before Jefferson or any of his entourage arrived. It was difficult to rationalize away his possessiveness about the house, to leave it and to leave the things in it. The Adamses were the first "first family" to live there, and in it Adams felt that he was the best version of himself. It is unlikely that he could pack away his feelings with his personal possessions. He might have found a modicum of satisfaction had he been able to take a mental leap over Jefferson and find the house alive with future generations of presidents. Had he known that his son John Quincy would be among them, he would have enjoyed the leap a great deal more.

John Adams did not like the people's choice for the next resident. It hung the unwelcome portrait of Thomas Jefferson front and center on the inner walls of his psyche. This image offended his mind's eye. John Adams's image of himself would need to be rehung somewhere else.

His mind crowded with images as his feelings followed his eyes toward the end of their farewell tour—and the fact of his loss sank into the very architecture of his life. There were many losses associated with this time: his career, his sense of himself, and more, but Jefferson made a good target. He was right there in the moment, and Adams displaced most of his feelings from the whole confluence of events into temporary housing at Jefferson's expense.

When the door of the White House closed behind them, Adams and the others maneuvered their burdens to the coach stop in the dark. Their path was slippery where broken rocks had been pressed and fitted, then mortared with now frozen mud.

The sky was clear, though rain was expected to alternately slush, then freeze the roads along the way. It would be uncomfortable when they jounced about on icy ridges and ruts left along the route by other horses and carriage wheels.

The prospect of a lengthy, bone-jangling trip was miserable. Adams had long since learned to endure his often iffy physical condition, but an achy, painful trip was certain. In his diaries and letters over the years, complaints about various aches and pains pop up as transient impediments in an otherwise healthy man. But although he regularly expressed concern that his health would interfere with his work, the record of his activities would seem to demonstrate that the health concern itself simply needed to be conveyed to others to give him some relief and settle the matter for the time being. He needed someone or something to receive and contain his physical complaints. This solution worked well for him. His wife accepted it. Colleagues found it one more way in which Adams could be annoying. Benjamin Rush suggested once more that he do some writing as a method for soothing the mind, but generally Adams preferred the oral complaint method. For the most part, his capacity to think and work was uninterrupted by his preoccupation with his health.

Adams was not a man to walk away both beaten and silent, any more than he would have walked away from his perceived duty because of a perceived illness. Not a passive fellow when faced with obstructions, his mind turned to solutions. He decided to try writing after all, thinking it might help him feel better if he wrote for publication. He hoped some of his ideas for the second term would work their way into the public mind, then into action by means of the people's influence. But even in the doing of it he felt uninspired and unsatisfied. He continued his diary, worked unenthusiastically on his autobiography, wrote and received hundreds of letters in correspondences with many, many people. Still unsatisfied, he conveyed his frustration to Rush in a letter; Rush recommended that he continue the effort. Adams responded, "You advise me to write my own life. I have made several attempts, but it is so dull an employment that I cannot endure it."[7]

The 4 o'clock coach departed eight hours before Jefferson's inauguration and move into the White House. Adams would not be there for either event. His absence caused quite a stir in the media. Commentaries ranged from saying that he was a sore loser slinking off in the night to disappointment that he had not demonstrated a point of pride in the new democracy, the smooth and peaceful transition of government. Another interesting possibility remains unknown: whether Adams was even invited to, or expected to attend, the inauguration. There was as yet no precedent.

On the day he was told that he had lost the election, Adams received word that his son Charles, age thirty, had died. Charles's wife and baby daughters were staying with Abigail, and Abigail had not been well during the last several months. Adams was in bad shape while he waited, anxious to be on his way. There had been no time for a break in fast pace during the closing days of his presidency to take it all in. His journey home would parallel his journey inward. But the inward journey would take longer. Happily, he would find a companion for that journey, though not for four more years. By means of their correspondence, Adams and Rush would examine the unknown, unconscious, sense-giving factors that influenced their lives. They would share their life stories and their dreams.

Adams's mind turned to thoughts of living in his own house, having time with family and friends, the physicality and pleasure of working the farm, and returning to his beloved library. Despite the reason for his departure, he was glad to be on his way.

Horses approached. The coach stopped. Gathering the stacked, tied bundles, they loaded the coach, climbed up and in. It was 4 a.m.

Senator Theodore Sedgwick, also on his way home, was in the coach. Adams must have been unhappy to see him. They had been political allies until a recent series of events had left each feeling betrayed by the other. Adams, expecting confidence and support in his negotiations with France, was disappointed that they were not forthcoming from Sedgwick, and Sedgwick, expecting to take part in the negotiations, was upset that Adams did not appoint him to the mission.

The problem between them reflected the insecurities and political tension generated by France's Bonaparte, who seemed to be out to conquer the world. He was already on the move, having taken Italy and Austria, and it was believed that he was planning to attack England, Egypt, and America with land and sea forces.

Adams's first plan in response to the perceived danger failed. In 1798 he sent envoys to try to conclude a treaty with France. They were detained by three bureaucrats in an extortion effort to solicit bribes in exchange for giving the mission an opportunity to have their official meeting. Having waited in France for six months, and having refused to pay the bribe, they did not get the meeting and came home empty-handed. The event, which Adams later called the XYZ affair (disguising the three French culprits' names), convinced Congress not to negotiate with France. Adams assured Congress that he would never send another mission to France without guarantees that their treatment would be appropriate.

Adams did not inform Congress that, following the XYZ affair, Elbridge Gerry, an envoy in the 1798 mission, had been told privately by Tallyrand, the French foreign minister, that he would only deal with Gerry. Tallyrand required that Gerry remain in Paris when the others went home, threatening that if he did not stay, the French would declare war on America. Gerry remained in France for a year of negotiations. Tallyrand forbade Gerry from explaining the situation to anyone in America except Adams—who was also sworn to silence. As a consequence, Gerry's reputation became the unfortunate subject of gossip at home, and Adams appeared, to his colleagues in government and to the voting public, to be doing nothing about France.

Upon Gerry's return in October he immediately notified Adams in a private conversation that the French were ready to conclude a peace treaty. In what seemed an impromptu about-face, Adams interrupted the Senate to have Vice President Jefferson read a formal request to send a mission to France to conclude a new treaty. Adams did not explain himself or the circumstances. Jefferson, who was required to read the request to the Senate, was dumbfounded. He, along with many others, thought Adams had lost his mind. They remembered how the Americans had been treated on the last mission to Paris. There had been further outrages since then. French frigates were spotted not far off the coasts of several southern states. War at sea was already under-way. The American warship *Constellation* had been taken by the French frigate *L'Insurgent* in March. In view of their reaction to Adams's request, it is surprising that Congress approved the mission. At first, Sedgwick supported the idea of a new mission, but he was soon swayed by the controversy it generated. Unaware of the confidential negotiations, he had no way to understand why he was not consulted or nominated to go on the mission. He felt disrespected and betrayed, and he exercised his displeasure by maligning Adams. Of the decision to send the mission, he wrote that Adams was vain, jealous, half-frantic, and ruled by caprice alone.[8] It was primarily because of his public and personal attacks on Adams, not his disagreement with the plan, that Adams felt betrayed by Sedgwick.

There would be plenty of time to find a middle ground for rela-tionship with Sedgwick during the long ride home, and it would have been Adams's style and nature to have done so. Adams was accustomed to differences of opinion, but he was not known to allow friendships to fall away without an effort to clear up personal affronts or misunderstandings. He had a lively sociability in his nature and a natural acceptance of human imperfection—even his own—when he recognized it. His relationship with Jefferson is the most notable exception.

The 1799 mission concluded a peace treaty with France in November, just prior to the election. Perhaps it would have made a difference in Adams's bid for reelection had the people known the whole story. But by the time the news that the mission was a success crossed the Atlantic, the election was over.

With hardly a poke in the air by the coachmen, the horses leaned into the job of moving them off. First to Baltimore—one day with the early start. From there, across rivers and through wilderness and forests, part of the journey in a violent storm, the five-hundred-mile trip home would take two weeks or so.

The trip to Massachusetts offered some small extraverted entertainments as well. Adams always enjoyed the overnight stops at inns and taverns even if he arrived with dampened spirits. He liked being caught up in the noise, smells, music, conversation, and fireside ambience of everyday life throughout the countryside. Adams was curious about citizens' thoughts on matters of particular interest to them and how those matters were being handled. A good conversation about religion or ethics or farming earned notes in his diary. He loved being recognized. A gregarious and outgoing fellow, Adams struck up conversations wherever he went. He loved food and waxed poetic in his diaries about special meals, particularly desserts and wines, but even a good pot roast or special pudding made the diary. He was familiar with the best cooks from here to there, and he knew who set the finest tables. Adams would stray for miles in an evening to enjoy good food and good company. He expanded on his new thoughts, generated by these conversations, in the diaries. But in reading them, it becomes clear that most of all Adams worried the pages with concerns for the future of his country.

Benjamin Rush attended Jefferson's inauguration but had to leave for Philadelphia as soon as possible. He left Washington while Adams was still en route home. His early start in March meant bitter cold, air as thin as a mountaintop, demanding exertion and pressured breathing. It exacerbated the exhausting effects of his "annual winter disease of the lungs."[9] The fastest way home was on horseback. Among the reasons for his hurry were that his wife was nearly due to have a child, and there was early confirmation of a new outbreak of yellow fever in the city.[10]

Rush was already worn thin on the sore subject of yellow fever, and he knew he was riding into a continuing storm on that account. There were only very primitive methods, all experimental, for treating it. Having suffered the disease and treated himself for it three times, he felt he understood how best to deal with it. But a mean-spirited controversy raged among physicians about what might be the best treatment for yellow fever. Rush received accolades and awards from heads of state in Europe for his work in dealing with the disease, but their praise made the sting of disagreement and lack of appreciation at home all the worse for him. Only four years before, a group of his American peers who were critical of his methods had given some negative interviews to the newspapers. As a consequence Rush sued the newspapers for libel. Although he won the lawsuit, bitterness burrowed into his personality. He resigned from the company of the College of Physicians only to find himself alone in a bleak professional vacuum. Newspaper coverage of the case cost Rush most of his medical practice, so his income suffered a radical decline. He then applied for a teaching position in New York, but the combination of political and medical enemies thwarted that possibility. When his financial condition had deteriorated to the point where he was uncertain he would have enough income to take care of his family, he told Adams about it. Adams appointed him to a job at the Mint, which provided Rush with a minimal income while he rebuilt his practice. It reconfirmed his lifelong appreciation and affection for John Adams.

He rode with his pouches stuffed to the brim with medical equipment, political homework, plans, papers, research for the medical school, and segments of the current book and articles he was writing.[11] There was no real road to speak of, but what there was would be hard packed and carved up with frozen wagon grooves and small ankle-breaking hoof hollows to watch out for. If it warmed up later in the day, the floor of the forest itself would yield to the months of soaking and trees would topple, sometimes blocking the entire passage. With a sharp eye, some hard riding, and the weather holding, Rush arrived home that very night.

In short order he was stretched thin between seeing patients, teaching duties, writing, and family matters. In addition to his professional writing, Rush also kept a diary and recorded his dreams, corresponded with his wife, and maintained working relationships and correspondences with Thomas Jefferson, James Madison, and others. The job at the Mint meant that Rush had to continue his difficult commute between Washington and Philadelphia. Fortunately, his new publications regenerated his reputation and his medical practice over the next four years.

John Adams at Home

Two weeks after leaving the White House, Adams's coach arrived in Boston. The sunlight, already folded into the thickening snow-fall, dimmed along with most of the light from the liminal moon. It would have been utterly silent in the deep snow were it not for the rattle of harnesses and horses, their great breaths steaming out into the ether. A storm was on its way, signaled by the falling temperature and rising wind, howling and harried, sounding its way through the baffle spaces between falling snowflakes. The rich smell of salt air, sniffed deeply out of the turmoil over the bay and south shore, sinks into the memory of homebodies like Adams, arousing old sensibilities about reliable, gratifying warmth. Save for this familiar Boston seasoning, there was no welcoming ceremony for the second president of the United States.

His boxes, crates, and miscellanea were hauled down, then hoisted up onto a farm wagon for the short ride home.

His house sat at the foot of Penn's Hill, from the top of which Abigail Adams had watched the British fleet and the attacks on Boston, and the defeat and fleeing of the fleet. In those days British soldiers foraging along the roads between Penn's Hill and the river that flowed nearby commandeered food and shelter in the house and many other homes along the way. Citizens were lucky if that was the only pain inflicted on them. Through all of it Abigail found herself managing the farm, raising the children, and carrying on during her husband's absences. Adams was away from home during the forming of the nation for the better part of eleven years. Abigail joined him from time to time in London and New York, and then Pennsylvania and was with him for much of his time in office as vice president, and later as president.[12]

The family farm and houses, barn, and outbuildings were acquiring a wraparound wall as a result of a continuous state of construction that made the best use of free material at the eponymous "Stoneyfield."[13] Adams was born in the older of the two houses, an unpainted wood structure, typical of early New England homes. Solid, square, its doorway somewhat narrow, the house sits almost flush with the ground. The entry opens directly into the central room dominated by a large open fireplace. It is used for cooking, as a source of light in the early hours, and it is the only source of heat for the bedrooms that open to the central room. The old house still stands today. The newer structure, his home when he returned, is a two-storey house built to accommodate his expanded family. The heat in the new house was inadequate during the worst of wintertime, particularly upstairs in the bedrooms where there were no fireplaces. The family would wrap themselves in warm clothing and blankets, each of them likely to wear a soft sleeping cap in the evenings and to bed. A great deal of indoor time was spent together around the fire—preparing food, eating, sewing, children playing, reading, talking. The genius loci of the Adamses' family culture was to be found at the fireplace as it was in most New England homes.

The house was an unpretentious, utilitarian living space, and Adams loved being there with his family. Later he added on another section of rooms and fireplaces so that Louisa and John Quincy's children could live there when John Quincy was traveling as a result of his own political career. Through the years various family members moved in and out of the Adamses' rotating nest. To accommodate them there developed a warren of hallways, doors, and short staircases that expanded the structure, though it

FIG. 4 John Adams's home in Quincy, Massachusetts, near Boston. Photograph by Sheila Zarrow.

maintained its basically boxy exterior. The house itself was like a living entity.

There was little to distinguish the house from other people's homes—that being a distinction in and of itself, because Adams was Massachusetts's most distinguished resident. Other presidents' homes—Washington's Mount Vernon and Jefferson's Monticello—spoke volumes about their distinguished residents. Adams consistently maintained that he liked the unaffected style of his house, a preference that is very much in keeping with his personal style. It is likely that this preference served him well also because his purse was quite empty most of the time.

Adams dressed simply, in dark clothing, with no adornment save the buckles on a belt or shoes. Ordinary in appearance, and a bit stout in part because of his excellence in divining where a good meal and good wine could be found, he had a rather commonplace look about him. Here again, set between the tall, elegantly tailored, and impressive Washington and Jefferson, in life and in history, Adams had little of the outward persona that earned his colleagues an additional modicum of public admiration. Even today, as one's eyes move across the capital city from the iconic Washington Monument to the Jefferson Memorial, the line of vision is not interrupted by any acknowledgment of the short, brilliant, hard-working engine of independence; there is no monument for John Adams.

In their later correspondence, Adams and Rush discussed their annoyance that artists and historians were elevating the part played by some of the founders to proportions beyond their deserving, while overlooking others. Adams wrote, and it would be easy to believe him knowing his character, that the only real posterity lay in being remembered in people's minds, not in monuments. On the other hand, perhaps he would have liked a monument. It is well known that Adams's humility had its limits—these he expressed colorfully in his diary and to Rush, "The next step would be prayers to them: 'Sancte Washington, ora pro nobis,' etc." [14]

Adams arrived at his front door the first night of what seemed to be a major outing for the wind god Boreas. A nor'easter on a grand scale plowed in with rain that froze into sleet mixed with snow and winds so cold and wild that once the wagon and team were unpacked, everything was locked down. No one went out of doors for the next ten days, and inside the house it was hectic.

Adams's family had grown during the crucial years between 1776 and 1801, when he was most often away from home. Daughter "Nabby" had married and given birth to four children, though one died in its first year. Nabby's husband, Col. William Smith, was an unreliable sort who went missing for weeks, and sometimes for months, with no explanation and was not there to help. In due course he stopped coming home altogether. Nabby and the children lived with the Adamses. Charles's death apparently from the effects of alcoholism just before Adams came home left his wife Sally and their two young daughters in the Adamses' care. John Quincy's family would also live with the Adamses from time to time when John Quincy was away on political assignments abroad. Adams's son Thomas was married and had seven children, all of whom were born during Adams's lifetime (one died in its first year). All together, another ten grandchildren were born following Adams's return. He did not lack for companionship, responsibility, or affection at home with Abigail and their expanding family. Though he was not running a country, it was clear that Adams was not about to start a restful retirement. Including helpers, relatives, and friends, there were often as many as twenty people living with them.

Adams had financial concerns about sustaining the household. Not long before his return home, the Bank of London, which held Adams's savings, folded—a total loss for him. Presidents were not well paid, and former presidents were not paid at all. Adams had to consider how he could earn a living. He was accustomed to intellectual stimulation, struggling with people and ideas, politics at a hectic pace. He wrote, "The only question remaining with me is what shall I do with myself? Something I must do, or ennui will rain upon me in buckets. Stillness may shake my old frame... Rapid motion ought not be succeeded by sudden rest."[15] He had no interest in returning to a law practice, and even less interest in local political options. He did not know what to do with his political passions, and it was very difficult for him to redirect his energies.

Since Abigail had been able to maintain the farm and sustain the family through his long absences, he decided to farm. It was practical, and he had always found great satisfaction in farming. He would again. He already referred to himself as "Farmer John."

But this did not make up for the satisfaction of knowing himself as "Mr. President." He was angry, and he was depressed.

His mood sank to a new low when, within his first week home, the following letter came from Thomas Jefferson:

> *Th: Jefferson presents his respects to Mr. Adams and incloses him a letter which came to his hands last night; on reading what is written within the cover, he concluded it to be a private letter, and without opening a single paper within it he folded it up and now has the honor to inclose it to Mr. Adams, with the homage of his high consideration and respect.* [16]

Adams responded at once:

> *Sir, I have recd. your favour of March 8 with the Letter inclosed, for which I thank you... Had you read the Papers inclosed they might have given you a moment of Melancholly or at least Sympathy with a mourning Father. They relate wholly to the Funeral of a Son who was once the delight of my Eyes and a darling of my heart, cutt off in the flower of his days, amidst very flattering Prospects by causes which have been the greatest Grief of my heart and the deepest affliction of my Life. It is not possible that any thing of the kind should happen to you, and I sincerely wish you may never experience any thing in any degree resembling it.* [17]

Jefferson did not respond. Adams could not know that Jefferson would also find himself bereft of a child with the death of his twenty-five-year-old daughter only three years later. Abigail took it upon herself to write Jefferson on that unhappy occasion, but there was no further communication between Adams and Jefferson until Rush and Abigail engineered contact between them eleven years later.

In his second week home, a letter came from John Quincy and his wife Louisa in Berlin, announcing the birth of their first child. They named him George Washington Adams. Abigail wrote, "I am sure [John Quincy]... had no intention of wounding the feelings of... father, but I see he has done it."[18] Adams was disappointed to have been second to Washington even in his own little domain.

By the third week the storm was over, and the family could finally go about its business. Adams began by unloading some of his political frustrations into a series of articles that he sent to newspapers and journals throughout the country, and he initiated a series of correspondences with important figures in government and in a variety of fields of interest. An unexpected, but most gratifying, outcome of the exchange of letters was the opportunity to review the history of the Revolution through the eyes of the people who participated in it. Adams was concerned that history was already being misrepresented by politicians in order to inflate their contributions and for political cachet. Rush had a similar concern: he was so determined that his children learn about the Revolution from his point of view that he wrote a history of it for them.

That spring Adams put his shoulder, quite literally, to the plow.

For several years he worked daily, side by side with his helpers. In just two years, the farm was able to support the whole family and the helpers. Adams also oversaw construction and additions for housing his family on the property. While these occupations raised his spirits, a diminishing readership for his articles made publishers reluctant to publish them.

By the third year publishing, as a route for channeling his extraverted energy, was all but closed to him. But by then the outward pressure of his energies was no longer the sole driving force. A gradual easing of his mind brought with it a gradual change in his personality. He still had a great passion for world events, but his interest in the people he had known through the years and cared about grew with every letter. He came to know old acquaintances more informally, more fully, and more intimately. Adams was always frank, and now in this more openhearted context of establishing relationships for his old age, this characteristic lost its pressured and obnoxious valence and showed him to be simply a man who spoke his mind.

chapter three

Rush's Dream of Mercury

By the fourth year after his long ride home Adams had found his way back into civilian life, and then he wrote a letter to his old friend Benjamin Rush.

Dear Sir,

It seemeth unto me that you and I ought not to die without saying good-bye or bidding each other adieu. Pray how do you do? How does that excellent lady, Mrs. Rush? How are the young ladies? Where is my surgeon and lieutenant? [19]

Rush responded very soon.

My much respected and dear Friend,

Your letter of the 6th instantly revived a great many pleasant ideas in my mind. I have not forgotten—I cannot forget you. You and your excellent Mrs. Adams often compose a subject of conversation by my fireside. We now and then meet with a traveler who has been at Quincy, from whom we hear with great pleasure not only that you enjoy good health, but that you retain your usual good spirits, and that upon some subjects you are still facetious....

Many thanks to you for your kind inquiries...

I live like a stranger in my native state. My patients are

*my only acquaintances, my books my only companions, and
the members of my family nearly my only friends. The odious
opinions I have propagated respecting the domestic origin of our
American pestilence (yellow fever) have placed me permanently
in the same situation in Philadelphia that your political opinions
placed you for a while in the year 1775.*[20]

Benjamin Rush is generally less well remembered in our own times than John Adams, but he was a famous and highly respected figure in politics and medicine during his lifetime. It helps to know some of his background. He was about six foot two or three, trim and elegant in appearance. He had been in his early twenties when he met Benjamin Franklin—already a noted figure worldwide for his talents and outspokenness and in America for fomenting dissatisfaction about the extant ruling principles in government. Obviously impressed with Rush's intelligence, Franklin had taken him under his wing, advanced him the cost of medical school in Edinburgh and London, and introduced him to John Adams— who influenced him on politics and revolution.

Rush once recounted the story of his family's immigration to America in a letter to Adams. His grandfather described the forested landscape when they arrived—followers of William Penn, seeking religious freedom. The woods were as mysterious as any storybook primal forest. Populated by unfamiliar indigenous people, they were restlessly alive day and night with wolves, bears, snakes, animals to hunt, and animals that hunted them. As the settlers carved out their living space, felling trees, then resurrecting them as the family farm, homes, and churches, their imposition altered the living space of the inhabited forest. There followed a myriad of conflicts between those who were already there and those who came. Disrupted ways of life, broken agreements with the Native Americans, and the constant influx of settlers and expansion of settlements pushed Native Americans and animals

of the forest farther and farther away from the lands and tradi-
tions that were central to their survival. To the Native Americans,
for whom the very ground was part of their religious and cultural
inheritance, theirs was the loss of both womb and tomb of their
creation myth. They were backed into an apocalyptic future.

Two generations later when Rush visited the farm to show
his youngest son the place where he was born, he found that the
land was now very quiet in comparison to the early years. It spoke
more of chickens, lambs, cows, pigs, dogs, reapers, mowers, and
threshers than of wolves or bears or the uncultivated forest. Rush's
grandfather, John Rush, lived a harsh and humble life in the new
land, especially when compared to the cosmopolitan life he had
led in England as a captain in the military under Oliver Cromwell.
Rush's father, born on the farm, was a farmer and a gunsmith, his
wares very much in demand long before the Revolution.

Adams understood the archetype of rebirth in the generations
in Rush's story about the family and the farm. He found meaning
in the parallel between the slope from wildness to domesticity and
in the changes from generation to generation. Adams described his
own projection of how a similar downward gradient from clamor
to calm and, hopefully, to peace might occur in the generations of
his own family. He wrote that he and Rush in their generation had
to study war so that their children could study peace, philosophy,
and law, so that their children could study art and music, literature,
and science.[21]

By the time Rush was thirty years old, married, and on his
way to producing a large family, he had a going medical practice in Philadelphia, and he was teaching at the medical school,
was a member of Congress, and had signed the Declaration of
Independence as representative from Pennsylvania.

When America exploded violently into the war for independence, Congress appointed George Washington to be General
of the Armies, and Washington appointed Dr. Benjamin Rush

to be physician general. In no time at all, Rush was torn between urgencies of every kind. He was physician to George Washington, Thomas Jefferson, John Adams, and other notables, including Betsy Ross, who lived across the street from Christ Church, next door to the new nation's capital in Philadelphia. This particular church was a formidable presence during the debates about what the relationship between church and state would be in American government, and it makes a revelatory appearance in the first of the dreams that Rush sent to Adams.

There were outbreaks of yellow and bilious fevers in the capital, Philadelphia, and in many of the cities and field hospitals, and many of the outbreaks were widespread and, most often, deadly. Medical research and treatment of wounds and diseases were primitive by our standards, and although physicians did their best, success was an intermittent prize and failure a common outcome of treatment. Anytime Rush's treatments failed, in those nervous times, it brought him grief and anxiety because American physicians—"white coats"—lined up to take potshots at him. Meanwhile British redcoats lined up and shot down men in the field, who then urgently needed Rush and his staff to go wherever they were needed and to do whatever they could to help. Of great importance, he incorporated the idea that physical and psychological wounds are inseparable and should be treated with like attitude. It is the first instance of trying to steer medical practice in the direction of understanding the relationship between psyche and soma—free of bias against mental illness and various psychological manifestations during wartime. This is the early form of what was to become Rush's greatest contribution to the understanding and treatment of mental illness, his book *Observations*. The most unexpected of all Rush's recommendations to physicians and medics of the newly amalgamated Continental Army of the United States was that they have all patients who were able write down their dreams.[22]

During the war Rush was torn between his two equally demanding jobs at the time: politician and physician. He answered both callings with a sense of urgency. He could devote only a part of his attention to each and was therefore never fully satisfied with either. Rush admired his grandfather's and father's abilities to adapt and respond to the demands of the environment with determination and creativity, but he judged himself to be more inundated and conflicted by necessities than creative in response to them. His dreams during this period visually represent his internal struggles and show how he wrestled with them in his pressured mind. Creativity, genius, and inspiration were in his nature and made it possible for him to do both jobs while continuing to do research, writing, and participate in his family life. But other than when he was with his family, there are few indications that he was ever really comfortable or at peace with himself until he was well into his correspondence with Adams years after Adams left office.

Their early correspondence ran the gamut of topics and set an informal tone for the ongoing friendship. They had differing political views, and since Rush was a Jeffersonian, their letters tell us the story of the contentious issues of the times. At the same time the letters give us insight into what Adams and Rush thought about themselves—and one another. In a typical letter Adams wrote:

> *I have just now received your friendly letter of the 19th and rejoice with you sincerely in the welfare of your family...*
>
> *Now for the first part of your letter....my facetiousness, you know, was always awkward and seldom understood...They used to tell me I had a little capillary vein of satire, meandering about in my soul, and it broke out so strangely, suddenly, and irregularly that it was impossible ever to foresee when it would come or how it would appear....I know nothing of any facetiousness in myself. If it is ever there, it comes of itself; I hunt it not....*

Now for the latter part of your letter....I resemble you and
Sancho.[23] *I call for my levers and iron bars, for my chisels, drills,*
and wedges to split rocks, and for my wagons to cart seaweed
for manure upon my farm. I mount my horse and ride on the
sea shore....Notwithstanding all this, I read the public paper
and documents, and I cannot and will not be indifferent to
the condition and prospects of my country....I love the people
of America and believe them to be...deceived. It is the duty of
somebody to undeceive them.[24]

Adams felt that Jefferson deceived Americans into a false sense of
security by policies and legislation that did not take into account
the dangers to peace and security while Europe was again at war.

FIG. 5 *Christ Church, after van Gogh's* Starry Night, Jennifer Leigh Erickson.
Personal collection of the artist.

Rush responded:

In the conclusion of your letter you say it is the duty of every man who loves his country to step forth in defense of its institutions. To this paragraph, as far as it was intended to awaken me to exertion, I shall reply by giving you an account of a singular dream.

The Dream

I was going up Second Street in our city and was much struck by observing a great number of people assembled near Christ Church gazing at a man who was seated on the ball just below the vane of the steeple of the Church. I asked what was the matter. One of my fellow citizens came up to me and said, the man whom you see yonder has discovered a method of regulating the weather, and that he could produce rain and sunshine and cause the wind to blow from any direction. The instrument he used was a trident in his hand which he waved in the air, and called at the same time to the wind, which then blew from the northeast, to blow from the northwest. I observed the vane of the steeple while he was speaking, but perceived no motion in it. He then called for rain, but the clouds passed over the city without dropping a particle of water. He now became agitated and dejected, and complained of the refractory elements in the most affecting terms. Struck with the issue of his conduct, I said to my friend who stood near to me, "The man is certainly mad." Instantly a figure dressed like a flying Mercury descended rapidly from him, with a streamer in his hand, and holding it before my eyes bid me read the inscription on it. It was: "De te fabula narratur." ("The story is told of you yourself.") [25]

Rush continued, "The impression of these words was so forcible upon my mind that I instantly awoke, and from that time I determined never again to attempt to influence the opinions and passions of my fellow citizens upon political subjects."[26] Rush sent a copy of the dream to Adams who responded, "I admire the brilliancy of your invention when asleep...But [disagree with your conclusion. I]...began to doubt whether the devil had not mounted on the golden ball instead of an angel of light."[27] Then Adams quoted this poem:

> *The Truth is this: I cannot stay,*
> *Flaring in Sun-shine all the Day:*
> *For entre Nous, We Hellish Sprites*
> *Love more the Fresco of the Nights;*
> *And oftener our Receipts convey*
> *In Dreams, than any other Way."*[28]

Adams went on to write that Rush's conclusion was too reductive for a dream story of mythic proportions. It was more like those of Aesop or Phaedrus, and that in addition to the story being told to Rush for himself, the dream was more generally relevant as a story for all people. Adams suggested its message could as well have read *entre nous fabula narratur* ("the story is ours").

Rush had a deep connection to Christianity and to Christ Church in particular, which contained in its discipline the centerpiece of his own moral compass. According to its teachings the wind often represented the moving spirit of the god image as described in the Bible. The dream ego watched to see if the wind could be moved by the pagan forces called up by the man in the dream.

Christ Church was the most prominent church in Philadelphia, the capital city at the time. Many of the nation's founders were members, among them George Washington, Thomas Jefferson, and Benjamin Franklin. Franklin, apparently a literalist about "one nation, under God," held a fund-raiser to build the great cupola that raised the ball, steeple, and vane of the church just a bit higher than the seat of government at Independence Hall next door. All the central ordering principles of heaven and earth converge in the setting of this dream, making it, in Jung's terms, an archetypal dream. Among the elemental symbols that distinguish it are that it takes place at the birthplace of the nation, that wind and weather are involved in the experiment, and that Mercury appears bearing a message from mythos. Most of the dream's images have at least one foot in the world of 1790, when Rush was working on his theory that madness was a product of a disorder of the soul. He was also deeply involved in the design of democracy and in the discussion of the place of religion in the new government. Many parts of the dream have fairly clear associations to his daily life, the main exception being the figure Mercury, about which Rush made no comment.

In his work as a physician, Benjamin Rush was familiar with the irrational in its varied manifestations in his mental patients. He used the word *madness* interchangeably with the word *irrational*. Both words indicate the presence of what would later be called products of the unconscious. Rush used *madness* broadly to include the whole continuum of irrational thought, behavior, and nonlinear expression, as indicated by a disturbance of the mind, or its appearance in dreams. Rush concluded that the man in the dream must be mad because when the he fell to the ground he complained of "refractory elements" (untreatable conditions). That the man had been experimenting outside of the church led Rush to believe he had a disorder of the soul.

A conclusion of this sort was not unusual for Rush, whose observations convinced him that people were more susceptible to irrational influences during extremely stressful times.

Rush also found that there was a potential for irrationality in otherwise healthy persons such as himself—as evidenced by dreaming. He wrote that the potential for irrationality and madness is part of the human condition that when activated, puts the "soul out of balance"—producing the upshot dreams to discharge these effects. Rush took an experimental approach to this attempt to "cure" dreams: he had his patients write them down. Rush's writings offer no explanation of why or how it helped to write them down. He observed that writing his own dreams relieved and restored him, and that it helped his patients when they recorded theirs.

Having patients write their dreams was one of those inspirations that stumbles into unpredictable discoveries in much the same way that unmanned ships sometimes find their way to shore. What Rush intended was to stop the dreaming. What he accomplished was to begin an intentional relationship with the irrational by engaging it, rather than confronting or ignoring it. In the writing of it, the dream, an unsubstantial essence, was transposed into solid, literal form on paper in the waking world. By this action Rush found that he diminished the dream's power to involve the dreamer in the excitation of its irrational influence.

"Curing" dreaming seems counterintuitive to the modern eye—something like curing a symptom rather than its underlying cause. But the merit in Rush's "cure" of writing the dream down is more intuitive than counterintuitive. Although his idea that dreams are a product of a disorder of the soul is, in part, a product of Rush's religious background, there is a latent gnosis that jumps the times. His sense that a disturbance of the mind or body points to a disturbance in one's essential relationship with the divine was his first tentative step toward accepting that the psyche has a natural, inherent religious function and that this function was revealed in dreams.

Philosophy and religion cross-pollinated one another in the search for self-knowledge for centuries. When Adams's and Rush's ancestors immigrated to America, churches generally emphasized the idea of self-knowledge to serve a purpose related to redemption, rather than deepening the understanding of the human psyche. Rush's family arrived during the revival, by Descartes, of interest in a third-century idea, *gnothi sauton*.[29] There is a precious identity between *gnothi sauton* ("know thyself"), and *de te fabula narratur* ("the story is told of you yourself"), the expression that appeared in Rush's dream. During Rush's and Adams's lifetime, Kant expanded on the idea of self-knowledge to include the study of the nature of human beings as a whole. Adams's response to Rush's dream, *entre nous fabula narratur* ("the story is ours") is essentially Kantian. It focused less on redemption by a divine entity and more on people's responsibility to acknowledge and redress human conditions.

Rush's observations led him to speak, write, and encourage a change in attitude about irrational thoughts and behaviors to ensure kinder, gentler treatment than had been the practice in old England and new America. Rush saw mental illness without the stigma that generally attached itself to patients who were, until then, without a champion to speak on their behalf.

The man sitting on a ball of the church steeple in the dream was a centering image that gave a semblance of order and focus to the crowd in the courtyard. This is significant in much the same way that the setting of the dream at the nation's capital gave order and expression to a relationship between church and state, man and god, and their equivalents in psychology, ego and Self. All of these are structural mandalas, ordering principles that are very far-reaching. In Rush's dream the archetypal idea of universal order appears in many forms. The ball can be seen as a more familiar, less esoteric representation of a structural mandala, a model of the universe. Considering that later in the dream Mercury descends from beneath the man, it would seem that what he was "sitting on" contained the potential for new vision at a suprapersonal level.

Conducting his experiment, from up on the ball, the dream figure waved a trident and called on the wind to change directions.

The trident is a complicated and ambiguous symbol. The three strongest associations to the trident when paired with Christ Church in this dream are the devil (Satan), Poseidon (Neptune), and Christ. Associated with the devil it personifies autonomous psychological complexes that operate in the unconscious and are known to influence one's thoughts, feelings, attitudes, and behavior. Adams thought of them as "hellish sprites that work in the dark." Considering the man's experiment as a scientific one—conducted outside or upon the church—the trident as an instrument of the devil also represents the eighteenth-century attitude toward "the pernicious hubris of scientific thinking."[30]

FIG. 6 *Mercury/Hermes* (1580) by Giovanni da Bologna. Museo Nazionale del Bargello, Florence.

The trident was also known as the instrument with which Poseidon ruled the seas and subdued the Leviathan, a chthonic serpent or primitive snake form.[31] Subduing the Leviathan in the sea is the psychological equivalent of "refractory elements." It created a lockdown in the unconscious and blocked the symbol-making process so that a dialogue with consciousness was no longer possible. The north wind that the man summoned, most often associated with, and personified by, the primitive god-figure, Boreas, may also have contributed to his subsequent condition. There might have been a doubt about whether the wind called upon was the spirit of God or that of the devil were the question not answered both by the appearance of an unchristian god-figure, Mercury, and by positioning the man outside of Christ Church so that he is not contained within the idea of it. Boreas, who brings on the winter cold, is said to be harsh-tempered and devouring. Apparently offended by the arrogance of the man, Boreas soon devoured him in a winterlike condition. Locked in a frozen state he was beyond the reach of human medical intervention.

Jung wrote that in medieval allegory a golden trident was an allusion to Christ, its three hooks an allusion to the Trinity, and that primordial man was the bait for catching the powers of darkness.[32] Considered in terms of Rush's dream, the dream man would represent primordial man, an essential figure at the earliest stage of development. He was the bait. The powers of darkness, those elements of the unconscious that take the bait, essentially attach themselves to the least-developed aspects of the psyche. Fished from the sea of unconsciousness, they have the potential for transformation and development.

The ambiguity characteristic of symbols shows itself in the several possibilities of the trident motif, in the juxtaposition of Christ as fisherman with Satan, and again in the multiple watery ideas associated with Neptune. Dreams convey their essential message by means of insubstantial phenomena such as these, and they convey a sense of substantiality by assuming forms such as the man, Mercury, and the trident, whose seemingly real subsistence exert themselves against the resistance of conscious reason. One of the defining, albeit complicating, features of dreams is that their content can engender action that is based on the reality of the psyche but that may be at odds with reality in the outer world. Rush really wanted to quit government work, but two strong forces kept him going: his sense of moral obligation and the need for income from the job. Rush responded to the dream man as though he were a mirror image of himself, but Rush was caught in a much greater eternal drama than he imagined. Driven from pillar to post by the enormity of the archetypes of destruction and creation, in which he was one of the period's greatest pawns, Rush was sometimes inspired and energized and at other times depressed.

Mercury did not appear until the man descended, literally and figuratively, out of his inflated identity with powers greater than himself and down into his human feelings. Mercury held the message to the sleeping Rush's dreaming eyes rather than the climbing man's eyes, perhaps because the man had served his purpose and the messenger was ready to relate to Rush more directly.

One reason the dream seemed uncomplicated to Rush in making his decision to leave politics was that he based it on the first and last parts of the dream, the church climber's actions and the message on the streamer, leaving out the centerpiece and denouement: the impressive incarnation of a god figure depicted in the surprise descent of Mercury. Rush and Adams both noted the message but not the messenger.

The message was held to the dream ego's eyes as a mirror for reflection (consciousness). Rush was to understand that the man in the story was something of himself (*de te fabula narratur*). The point was that the eye must see the I. But Rush's first impulse upon waking was to reject this. He wanted to break from any chance of being like the man in the dream. He thought he could distance himself from his own story: "I determined never again to attempt to influence the opinions and passions of my fellow citizens upon political subjects." Rush did not notice that political subjects had little to do with the story that was told.

The man performed the experiment as if he were an alchemist, but like a dream within a dream, in fact, the experiment was performed on him in the vessel of Rush's dreaming mind. The man was the *prima materia*. He performed a challenge that had implications for potential change in people's beliefs about science, nature, and God. He did this as a symbolic, substitute agent for Rush, representing perhaps Rush's inferior function or shadow, or perhaps Rush was unconsciously questioning his own faith—and science—by projection onto the man. The dream not only drove Rush from politics, it focused his energies on medicine and psychiatry.

No one is certain why any particular mythic figure appears in a dream, but analysis demonstrates that there is usually an unconscious association between the figures in the dream and the dreamer. In this case the connection at the personal level is to Rush as a physician-healer. The eternal myth, synchronistic and making the connection with Rush's story, harkens back to a time when patients were treated by priest-healers. In 1200 B.C.E., they were called Asclepiadae, after the Greek god of healing, Asclepius (Roman, Aesculapius), and associated in Rush's generation, and now our own, with Hippocrates, a Greek physician, as the father of medicine. Mercury was his messenger. The symbols associated with the archetype remain unchanged—the caduceus (a form of the trident) with snakes entwined representing the potential for healing and renewal and wings recalling Mercury, carrier of messages. It is not at all uncommon for godlike forms to appear in dreams. Their elevated status and inherent characteristics represent the form, nature, pressure, and relative priority of the intrapsychic material in process. New ideas and attitudes must topple

FIG. 7 *Mercury/Hermes with cock and goat.* Artus Quellinus. Royal Palace. Amsterdam.

old dominant ruling principles in the psychic revolution. America's war for independence was a process parallel to the internal course of individuation—the battles fought for freedom and for consciousness are fought against the fortifications and rigid ethos of sovereignty.

The dream pressed Rush away from politics and toward medicine, psychiatry in particular. The agent of this change was Mercury, whom the Greeks earlier called Hermes, son of Zeus. While it appears that mythic figures collect new characteristics and change through time, even as their names change, the old characteristics cling to them as well. In his early Greek form as Hermes, Mercury was well known for doing things in reverse. For example, there is a story about his stealing a goat: while carrying it, he backed out of the scene of the crime walking on his own footprints to avoid being caught. It is like Hermes to lay in wait undetected, then descend abruptly from beneath the man in the dream. In this aspect Hermes is usually illustrated as a figure with an erect penis, symbolizing his potential to penetrate and impregnate the unsuspecting dreamer's mind. It is like Mercury to slip into that opening and as a go-between deliver a message from an immortal to a mortal being.

Rush's writings did not confirm that, by means of the dream, his psyche steered him away from politics purposefully in order to focus his energy on medicine. He wrote only that he was afraid that if he stayed active in politics, he would suffer the fate of the man in the dream.

A dream of Descartes has a motif similar to Rush's dream. In it a wind is blowing in the direction of the church, so the dreaming Descartes concluded that "it cannot be the wind that once filled the church, it had its origin not in the Church but outside it.... The church is no longer a vessel but, according to circumstances, either an obstacle on its path or a refuge for those who fear the wind."[33] Descartes was puzzled by this paradox: he interpreted the wind as "the evil spirit which tried to push him forcibly to a place where he wanted to go voluntarily," and he questioned whether "this wind was the spirit of God or the spirit of Satan, which was also thought to be a *ventus urens,* coming out of the North."[34]

In both Descartes's and Rush's dreams there was a shadow figure observing the scene, Rush's fellow citizen in the courtyard of the church, Descartes's man in the quadrangle at the church. In both dreams the seed for the emerging symbol was held in a structural mandala—in Rush's dream, the ball on which the man sat, and in Descartes's, a melon. Both dreamers diverted the shadow elements and the question of evil into conscious thinking and an impetuous outward flow of thoughts. In the course of the dreams' ascension from the unconscious world both dreamers considered the religious implications. Both took action motivated by the powerful visual terminology of their dreams. Descartes was redirected "back to dwell on himself and his own life," and Rush was referred back to himself, *de te fabula narratur.* Like Descartes, Rush believed the dream pushed him to a decision that he would have taken voluntarily.

One outcome of Rush's dream was that his energies were canalized in different measure—less supportive of his political interests and more supportive of his interests in medicine and psychiatry. The increased energy resulted, without Rush being aware of it, in a deeper study of his own shadow, as projected onto his patients. If Rush was correct that dreaming happened because one's faith was out of order, it would follow that perhaps his own faith was undergoing some challenges at the time of his dream.

The concept of faith is seen in two ideas about religion that the dream illustrates. The first is the most familiar: the God ideal as carried by, and associated with, religions and religious institutions. The second idea of faith is the less familiar psychological one: the God ideal is inherent in the human mind or psyche. Psychologically, the religious spirit can be accessed either way—by

FIG. 8 *History of Medicine* (1960), mosaic by Conrad A. Albrizio. University of Southern Alabama Hospital, Mobile, Ala.

means of institutions where one seeks God, or by establishing an interior relationship with the Self, as Rush is instructed to do in his dream. Known as the "religious function of the psyche" in Jung's analytical psychology, the analogical maxim is: man is to God as ego is to Self. The images found in the mosaic *History of Medicine* (figure 8) are a visual expression of this maxim. It shows the long intertwined history of the archetypal physician and the spiritual healer that drew Rush into a deep understanding of the relationship between spiritual and physical well-being. This connection expressed itself in his dream.

Hippocrates is shown in two forms at the center of the mosaic: in white robes representing the spiritual and in brown robes representing the physical. He is taking and administering the Hippocratic oath to doctors in temples where the sick gathered to worship and receive care. The winged mask above the brown-robed figure recalls the winged messenger, Mercury, who delivers the oracle, or the voices of gods. The Egyptian physician Imhotep (ca. 3000 B.C.), also an architect, scientist, and surgeon, is shown holding the triangle and scalpel symbolizing his professions. The feminine spiritual counterpart to Imhotep is the goddess Isis, imaged as the all-seeing eye and as animal behind him. Imhotep together with Isis represents the connection to both the spiritual and animal aspects of healing. As the image moves forward in history, the omniscience connected more closely with gods than human practitioners recedes. The Greek physician Galen of Pergamum (lower right) begins with the bare bones, learning by studying a human skull and taking notes. Vesalius (left front), a Flemish physician of the sixteenth century, is working directly with patients. Vesalius and Galen illustrate the comparatively recent differentiation of the practice of medicine out of its identity with the gods, although the legs of that differentiation continue to be a little wobbly in our own times. In Rush's eighteenth-century dream, the gods associated with the physician/healer archetype were deeply engaged with him as a human spokesperson through whom they issued their agency. This was the source of Rush's internal pressure, that is, his calling.

chapter four

Adams's "Annimatical" Dream

*I dreamed that I was mounted on a lofty scaffold in the center
of a great plain in Versailles, surrounded by an innumerable
congregation of five and twenty millions, at least, of the
inhabitants of the royal menagerie. Such a multitude is not to be
described or enumerated in detail. There were among them the
elephant, [the] rhinoceros, the lion, the hyaena, the wolf, the bear,
the fox, and the wildcat, the rat, the squirrel, as well as the calf,
the lamb, and the hare. There were eagles, hawks and owls of
all sorts, and storks and cormorants and crows, and ducks, geese,
turkeys, partridges, quails, robins, doves, and sparrows. There
were whales, sharks, dolphins as well as cod, mackerel, herrings,
and even minims and shiners.*

*My design was to persuade them to associate under a free,
sovereign, annimatical government, upon the unadulterated
principles of liberty, equality, and fraternity among all living
creatures. I had studied a long speech, arranged it in exact method,
with a beginning, a middle, and an end, with an exordium and
a very pathetic peroration, according to the most orthodox rules
of the most approved rhetoricians. Throwing my eyes round and
gracefully bowing to my respectable audience, I began:*

*"My beloved brothers! We are all children of the same Father
who feeds and clothes us all. Why should we not respect each
others' rights and live in peace and mutual love!"*

I had not pronounced all these words before the elephant pouted his proboscis at me in contempt, the lion roared, the wolf howled, the cats and dogs were by the ears, the eagles flew upon the turkeys, the hawks and owls upon the chickens and pigeons. The whale rolled to swallow twenty at a mouthful, and the shark turned on his side to snap the first he could reach with his adamantine teeth. In a word, such a scene of carnage ensued as no eye had ever seen and no pen or pencil ever described.

Frightened out of my wits, I leaped from the stage and made my escape—not, however, without having all my clothes torn from my back and my skin lacerated from head to foot. The terror and the scratches awakened me and convinced me forever what a fool I had been. [35]

The narrative in his waking life made its way into Adams's annimatical dream story in symbolic form. Adams wrote little of what he thought about the dream in his letter to Rush, except to say that "the father of us all" in the dream peroration was based on his belief that the "Christian religion was intended to give peace of mind to its disciples in all cases whatsoever... [but] sent a sword instead."[36] Adams and Rush understood that religion fell short of providing peace of mind for all people. In the dream the proposed peace plan failed, and the threat of the sword was symbolically represented by the scratches and cuts Adams suffered; *separatio* rather than *coagulatio* remained the order of the day in that dream.

Upon receiving the letter with the dream enclosed, Rush wrote Adams,

My Venerable and Dear Old Friend,
My whole family was delighted in contemplating you upon your rostrum in the garden of Versailles and in witnessing the effects of your speech upon your hairy, feathered, and scaly audience. Let it

not be said, "De republica America fabula narratur."
("The story is told of the American republic.") [37]

Adams had dreamed the dream twenty-two years before he wrote
it down and sent it to Rush. Back when he dreamed it he had not
yet had the many discussions with Rush about what was to be
gained by recording his dreams. But by now Adams considered
dreams (and the unconscious) a source of knowledge—so when he
revisited the dream to share it with Rush, he was much more delib-
erate and interested and was looking for what the dream had to
say to him. With amazing clarity of mind, our pre-Jungian Adams
concluded that there are mythic elements in dreams such as this
one that are well beyond the ken of most of the individuals who
dream them. He wrote that some dreams are therefore equally relevant as stories for the collective and the culture as well as for the
individual. He wrote to Rush that indeed, the story is told of the
American republic: *Entre nous fabula narratur* ("the story is ours").
Synchronistically, Rush's dream of the man climbing the church
was also an old dream from the same year, 1790, and similarly had
not been recorded until he sent it to Adams. There is a timeless-
ness about archetypal dreams that shows them to be living things,
set aside for the time being, then called back into participation in
the life story of the dreamer.

If, as Rush believed, dreams were caused by aggravating stim-
uli, 1790 was the perfect year for dreaming. John Adams had just
become America's first vice president the year before. Of his job,
Adams wrote to his wife Abigail, "My country in its wisdom contrived for me the most insignificant office that ever the invention
of man contrived or his imagination conceived." [38] But the appar-
ent lackluster of his position did not last long. Conditions in the
world of 1790 slumped into a serious declension from bad to worse.
In April, Benjamin Franklin died. He was revered as though he

were a permanent architectural post supporting the national structure. The nation was shaken to its foundations. The next month, President Washington fell gravely ill and was removed to his home in Virginia. His doctors thought he might die of pneumonia. Abigail Adams wrote,

> *At this early day when neither our finances are arranged, nor our government sufficiently cemented to promise duration, his [Washington's] death would, I fear, have [the] most disastrous consequences. Most assuredly I do not wish for the highest spot. I never before realized what I might be called to do, and the apprehension of it only for a few days greatly distresses me.* [39]

Adams despaired that he was "only one breath away from disaster." [40] In May there followed an epidemic of influenza that left Madison and Jefferson so ill that they had to go home. Many others in government fled the capital to wait it out. The situation worsened before June, as pockets of yellow fever broke out in several cities and Rush was called away to serve in his capacity as a physician wherever he was needed. With so many key people— the founding fathers, whose presence would ordinarily have had a stabilizing effect—not present to conduct the business of government, Adams's responsibilities and angst rose.

During this same time the French Revolution was percolating, with consequences that were felt throughout Europe. This brew added to America's collective uncertainty about the future. Two immediate concerns were that a disturbance in trade could unravel the frayed American economy and that an unexpected but potential invasion by any nation would threaten the country's survival.

America still had no way to protect its coasts. Adams continued to argue and fail in his efforts to develop a navy to protect America from invasion. One reason he failed was that the country was broke, having incurred about twenty-five million dollars in debts during the Revolution. The states had had to pay their own way during the war. An effort was made by Hamilton to solve the debt problem. He proposed that states' debts and those of the central government be taken on as a national debt. This "Assumption Plan" was defeated in Congress but succeeded in aggravating the bad feelings between the North and South, which had very different debt liabilities. North and South were also divided over issues of slavery and, at this most inopportune time, came the added issue about where the capital of the country should be.

Just as in his dream Adams was working on unifying issues between various species, in his waking life he was deeply involved in the creation of the Bill of Rights, a series of ten amendments to the Constitution. It was hoped the amendments would be responsive to the needs of the individual states and would fill in what they saw as missing from it. The Constitution, coupled with the Bill of Rights, would be a container large enough to hold a union of the opposites—individual differences and collective identity.

Adams hoped the Bill of Rights would make signing the Constitution more likely. Enmities within and between the states and division between the Federalists and anti-Federalists threatened to upend the entire process. Adams put his mind to helping facilitate Constitutional conventions in many of the states during the years 1789 and 1790, the year of the dream and year that preceded it. The application of conscious effort helped to work around and avoid the dreaded rout that occurred in his dream. The Constitution was signed in 1787, and the Bill of Rights was ratified in 1791. The dreaded rout later became the Civil War.

The annimatical government plan ran along in an unconscious parallel beneath the waking world above, making its way into Adams's dream story in symbolic form. In it, the dream ego set out to persuade an audience of disparate intrinsic qualities to form a government that would benefit all living creatures. *Annimatical* is an invented word. It combines the Latin *animalus* ("having breath of life") with the suffix "-matic," from the Latin *matical* ("self-acting" or "self-animated").[41] The qualities of the roots of the word *annimatical* exert powerful unconscious influences because their visual language in the dream seemed and felt like ferocious, physical, conscious reality. A sovereign annimatical government in Adams's dream represents a living, self-activated, internal pressure to unite, within Adams himself, divergent sovereign governing forces. Analytically, that which is annimatical is a living symbol of the activated Self.

As a setting in the psyche, a foreign country in a dream generally represents something at a distance; analytically, it represents someplace in the unconscious—at a distance from consciousness. Versailles was built for royalty in France, and there was, in fact, a very special menagerie collected by Louis XVI at Versailles during the time of Adams's dream. The king was very much out of order, and his kingdom was on the brink of revolt. He was voracious in his consumption of alcohol, conquests, and acquisition of possessions. His menagerie of exotic creatures was for show rather than for study, preservation, or education. A French newspaper chided the king for seeing the menagerie as "a symbol both of his global reach and of the potency of his will."[42] The papers lampooned him, writing that he "represented a big animal nature—created with regret."[43] Under Louis XVI, Versailles itself became an international emblem for psychic disunity. Most of the exotics in the menagerie represented entreaties or peace offerings from nations he threatened. He also ordered specific exotics for his collection. All were similarly bound, packed, and shipped without regard for preservation, mates, special needs, climate, foods, or space. Jammed into the interstices not otherwise occupied by supplies and cargo, they shared a similarly abominable journey to hell with slaves who were chained below decks nearby.

It cannot be supposed that the breakup of the gathering of the menagerie in the dream was a simple rejection of the "father of us all" in favor of a return to Mother Nature. Members of the menagerie were not free to go. They could not return to their natural habitat. The answer lies in closer parallel to the American revolutionary experience: the psychic cure for the psychic problem of the paradox of the eternal troubled present is not a return to the past. The cure may lie in revolution. Perhaps this is why Adams wrote that the father "did not send civil or political peace upon earth but sent a sword instead."[44] That thought was represented by something at the cutting edge of the genius of the psyche that placed Adams's dream ego on a scaffold to give his speech. The implication of the guillotine inherent in the connotations of the word *scaffold* was that his head, lost in rhetoric, was separated from his heart and so his life was threatened.

The dream instructed that the menagerie was "not to be described or enumerated in detail"—in other words, it was to be considered as a unit of one. It is problematic to devise equality by uniting opposites that are each, in their own way, already whole. To the individual members of the captive menagerie, Adams's dream ego's offer of an annimatical government may have seemed more like trading one master for another rather than like a true vision of an equable government. One philosophical description of a new entity that has the potential for containing the opposites without destroying their disparate natures is the golden mean.[45] Another is described in the unusual math of alchemy in the Axiom of Maria, in which $1 + 1 = 3$, meaning one opposite combined with another single opposite results in a third thing or whole new concept that is neither the one nor the other. The third accomplished is known as *vir unus*.

The combustion at the end of Adams's dream brought him down from the inflation of his peroration and into his feelings, reconnecting his head and his heart. In the figurative language of alchemy, psychic disunity and inner chaos are likened to herds of animals and become the *vir unus* (the unified man) when the contradictory feeling values they represent are integrated. This "quest for consciousness is against nature and exposes the individual to reprisal."[46] The scratches and lacerations Adams suffered were the remnant penetrations that would immunize him against future attacks. Adams wrote, "The terror and the scratches awakened me and convinced me forever what a fool I had been."

Adams was no fool. After the annimatical dream he changed his working tactics. Recognizing that his approach and manner were often off-putting, even if his ideas were good, he took to rerouting his delivery. On particularly divisive issues he began, more often, to approach and convince individuals who represented a union of attitudes similar to his own. He set about getting them to present the ideas to Congress instead of doing it himself. He began to develop some finesse at getting his ego out of his own way.

The annimatical dream should not be considered solely in the context of when it was dreamed, the year 1790. It was not brought fully into the world until Adams recollected it and sent it to Rush. The influence of the twenty-two-year gestation may add another layer to its meaning. This dream ripened for the picking in 1812, the year in which Adams had the theater dream, which appears to be something of a bookend to this one (see chapter 6).

Rush's letters continued to provide an essential conduit for information to reach Adams in his relatively distant home—so far from the political center that throughout Jefferson's time in office and the onset of the War of 1812, the delay in receiving news was a hardship and caused Adams anguish for which Rush had great empathy. The fate of the country was too often in the balance. Because of Rush's continuing activities and relationships in Washington, he was privy to news, backroom intrigues, plans, the inner workings of government—and he kept Adams informed as promptly as he could.

Adams's preoccupation with world events continued, but it was the personal addenda to Rush's newsy letters, and Adams's responses in kind, that led to the evolution of a warm and friendly kinship. To little stories about life and family, opinions, and a variety of complaints, they added, with shared annoyance, that they both deserved and wanted more public and historic recognition than they were getting.

Though Adams felt that the drastic increase in physicality in his life (that is, farming) aggravated his sore, aging body, his complaints by mail did not provide the immediate gratification or relief that he used to get when he complained in person. The old method—complaining to someone, feeling better, and moving on—was replaced by reflective moods and thoughts about his life and legacy. Instead of extraverting the difficulties of the somatic life he so undervalued—as compared to his intellectual life which he valued highly—he gradually became accustomed to living with his discomforts for longer periods of time. He reflected on them, and this reflection appears to have helped him become more phlegmatic about them. The ever-deepening friendship with Rush allowed him to write to Rush without unloading the aches and pains as disowned physical conditions. In due course he developed an uncomplicated acknowledgment of them and accepted the impediments as inconveniences to get around as best he could— these matters were reduced to small items in his letters. This alteration in attitude is evident in this letter he wrote to Rush:

> *I sleep well o'nights; no burdens, whether grasshoppers or mammoths of body or mind, affect me. I still enjoy a chair in this study, but avoid close thinking from principle... So much for the bright side.... And now I shall turn my thoughts from this good humored small talk to the angry, turbulent, stormy science of politics.* [47]

The public reverence Washington was receiving left Adams feeling envious, irritable, and unappreciated. He wrote to Rush that Washington's talents were gaining

> *immense elevation... Talents!.... you will say, what talents?*
> *I answer. 1. An handsome face.... 2. A tall stature... 3.... an*
> *elegant form. 4. Graceful attitudes and movements. 5. A large,*
> *imposing fortune... there is nothing, except bloody battles and*
> *splendid victories, to which mankind bow down.*[48]

Rush replied that great men have neither ancestors nor posterity but are participants in an activated principle of faith synchronistic with their own times.

Consistent with that thought, Rush never lost his negative feelings about George Washington, whom he thought was more interested in posterity than in the urgent existential medical needs of his armies—delays and absence of supplies cost one third of the wounded soldiers their lives. The pain of Rush's impotence as physician general to provide for his doctors and patients in the absence of supplies fell heavily on his shoulders. He wrote that Washington's neglect was a moral betrayal of the faith America had placed in him.

FIG. 1 *Gabriel Weather Vane (Technique)*
(1939) by Lucielle Chabot. National
Gallery of Art, Washington, D.C.

FIG. 2 *John Adams* by Gilbert Stuart.
National Gallery of Art, Washington, D.C.

FIG. 3 *Benjamin Rush*, portrait by
Charles Willson Peale after painting
by Thomas Sully. National Historical
Park, Philadelphia.

(above)

FIG. 5 *Christ Church, after van Gogh's* Starry Night (2010), by Jennifer Leigh Erickson. Personal collection of the artist.

(below)

FIG. 8 *History of Medicine* (1960), mosaic by Conrad A. Albrizio. University of Southern Alabama Hospital, Mobile, Ala.

FIG. 11 Capture of the H.B.M. Sloop of War *Frolic*, Captain Whinyates, by the U.S. Sloop of War *Wasp*, Captain Jacob Jones, after a close action of 43 minutes, October 18, 1812. Aquatint in colors, drawn and engraved by F. Kearny from a sketch by Lieut. Claxton of the *Wasp*. Courtesy of Beverley R. Robinson Collection, U.S. Naval Academy.

FIG. 13 *Sarah Siddons* (1793), shown at a monument to
Shakespeare in her role as Lady Macbeth. Portrait by
Sir William Beechey. National Portrait Gallery, London.

FIG. 15 *Thomas Jefferson* (ca. 1821),
portrait by Gilbert Stuart. National
Gallery, Washington, D.C.

FIG. 16 *Gabriel Weather Vane* (1939),
by Lucille Chabot. National Gallery
of Art, Washington, D.C.

Rush's Poem "After a Night of Perplexing Dreams"

During the Revolutionary War supplies were to be sent to the field hospitals by the various states, but this required pressure and pleas to Congress. Rush pleaded with George Washington to ask the states for help, and when Washington would not do it, Adams did what he could to wheedle food, medicine, clothing, and arms for the soldiers. But the states were each looking out for themselves. This was a time before the unification into a single military force, the Continental Army. Rush traveled from battleground to battleground and from disaster to disaster to disaster. He sank into a terrible, weary depression as his charges bled, froze, and starved for want of simple supplies.

When George Washington failed to act, Rush resigned his commission and criticized him and Congress for the "near-criminal neglect of the sick and wounded."[49] To Rush, Washington became a symbol of vested interest, ignorance, and bungling. Later Rush accused him of encouraging hero worship.[50] Rush became irritable at every stage of his discussion with Adams, who agreed with him, about the construction of a monument to Washington. Feelings did not subside easily for Rush. His resilience waned. The effect on him of his experience at the battlefields was insidious. One can get a sense of it in his poem.

After a Night of Perplexing Dreams

Where was my gentle guardian, where
When Spirits malignant of the air
(Press'd) Thro the Silence of the night
My soul unguarded to affright
And dar'd prophane with screams, my mind
When Sleep my reason had Confined.

. . . .

(Say) did'st thou seek thy native Skies
To breathe the pure celestial air
And join thy Kingdom spirits there
For there in envy blissful grove
They tune their harps to notes of love

. . . .

dull mortality appears
To keep my soul a prisoner here
Confined to earth escpos'd to foes
Who seek to poison my repose
With vain unprofitable dreams
Of Idle Joys and airy Schemes.[51]

The poem juxtaposes the opposites, the cherished image of the absent gentle guardian against a hostile image, malignant spirits in the air. If the guardian, as an anima or soul image, is the part of himself that he felt slipping away, then his body's experience would be that it must soon follow. Surrounded by death and dying and helpless to provide the necessary medical treatments, Rush became so desolate that even breathing the air seemed deadly.

The interior effects on his psyche multiplied in equal measure to the gravity and gore of his daily life on the fields. The malignant spirits against which the anima is juxtaposed are frightening, split-off fragments of Rush's shadow that seem to make him regret his dull mortality and wish he could escape the earth. He fell into a deep depression.

Another interior disintegration would not be visible to the naked eye: the gradual dissipation of an important sense-making function in his mind, his intuition. It was highly developed and served Rush well in anticipating otherwise unseen and unknown factors—this is known to have inspired him to new ideas and innovations in his field. If the gentle guardian of the poem also refers to his intuition—which had gone ahead, as is its nature, to the blissful grove, that is, to the place where intuition conceives the world (a sort of Eden)—what would guide him in the disturbing world of the battlefield? Rush felt left behind in the present. In the poem he called this existential dilemma "being left in prison." It was a condition reminiscent of the "refractory elements" in his earlier dream.

Rush did not confide all these feelings to Adams but found relief in corresponding more frequently and more informally. It was clear from the start that Rush had an unstinting respect for John Adams and that Adams held Rush in his highest regard. But their mutual affection became more genuine as many of their projections fell away and they really got to know one another. Adams was no longer the one-dimensional famous personage Rush respected because of his accomplishments. He became the fuller story of a human being with a family, personal concerns, books he liked to read, books he did not want to write. Setting aside his own aversion to political participation, Rush reported regularly and generously to Adams about politics. One benefit to Rush in doing so seems to have been that he enjoyed the community of intellectual interaction that the letters stimulated between them. The interest often extended to include the reactions of their wives, children, and friends to entertaining stories one or the other had written.

Rush wrote to Adams of the division between political parties, nascent during Adams's election but later quite pronounced. The following letter was of the sort that Adams cherished.

Our country is divided into two great parties called
Federalists and Democrats. The former are subdivided into
British Federalists, tory-Federalists, and American Federalists.
The latter are divided into French Democrats, Irish Democrats,
and American Democrats. They all hold different speculative
opinions in government and different views of the proper mode
of conducting public affairs. Suppose a ship to be manned by
sailors of six different nations, and suppose no one of them to
understand the language of the other. Suppose the ship to be
overtaken by a storm, and the captain and mates to be able to
speak the language of but one class of the sailors. What do you
suppose would be the fate of that ship? Is not this the exact
situation of our country? [52]

This letter was typical of the extraordinary matters that describe the men and the times. Adams extraverted the energy they generated in him, enthusiastically writing to others to rally support or opposition and getting others involved. Rush was different. He had two outlets, but only one of them was a relief to him. The first, his participation in government, made it possible to extravert his ideas directly—but it was not supported by his nature and thus was an unsatisfying and unrewarding outlet for him. His primary relief was found in the correspondence with Adams. Just as Adams had dumped his aches and pains on Rush, Rush now dropped off his concerns at Adams's door. Adams would act on them to the degree that he was able, or wished to, or he would dispute them. Either way, Rush was uplifted by the interchange that would ensue. He wrote to Adams:

While I thus open my heart to my dear old friend in complaints
against many of my fellow citizens, do not suppose that my
life has been made completely miserable by them. The good
I have enjoyed in Philadelphia…has far exceeded the evil I
have suffered. I have been blessed with an excellent wife and
affectionate as well as intelligent and worthy children. I have
had the constant and faithful attachment and support of half a
dozen…citizens…One of them [Adams] opened his purse to me
at the time when the publications against my practice reduced
the income from my business…I have been engaged with
ineffable delight in forming a new arrangement of facts in order
to derive from them new principles and new modes of treating
diseases. For these and all God's other mercies to me, I desire to
be truly, sincerely, and forever thankful.[53]

Rush's balance sheet between complaints and blessings is a window
into the great, good heart of a feeling man. He had developed a
method for encouraging internal dialogue between his mind and
body long before Adams turned from extraverting to reconciling
the two. His method included recording his dreams and examin-
ing them in relation to his everyday life and his health in an effort
to understand why he was having the symptom (that is, a dream).
Dreams and dreaming troubled him because they were ongoing
reminders that all was not well—that the balance in his mind was
unreconciled. Having concluded that there was an essential similarity between dreams as symptoms indicating the presence of a
problem and physical symptoms, such as pain or coughing that
point to causal conditions or syndromes, Rush might have incorporated these ideas into his practice. But he did not. He proceeded
as if the two were different processes.

Rush found solace in writing poetry. It was one of his personal
cures for dreaming—he used it as a dream catcher. Some of the

most transient of images floating freely in and out of his mind (dream or other matters) could be caught in a word net—the captive was then transposed from its airy form to word images in fluid ink, which dried, marrying it to the paper. Held still, the images and ideas were more readily accessible for conscious consideration. Writing poetry brought relief when Rush's mind was churning.

In his description of active imagination, Carl Jung recommended establishing an inner dialogue in much the same way that Rush found so helpful, that is, writing in order to transpose something internal and ephemeral into an external, more stable form. This is not the same as writing to communicate with another person. Jung referred to the internal entities with whom one had this sort of interchange as aspects of the Self. When the psyche inspires a dream, painting, music, poem, or other creative expression, fanciful or serious, the product arrives in the native tongue of the unconscious. Its language is symbolic and often appears in irrational rather than rational or literal form. "Irrational" in this context means, simply, not yet understood by the rational, conscious mind.

Rush practiced a form of active imagination throughout his lifetime—jotting poems on random sheets of paper that he tucked into books and drawers, unkempt. Because most of these jottings were not part of his diary or included in his books or correspondence, it would seem their purpose was served by his internal experience in the course of creative expression. Writing down his dreams gave Rush a sense that he was setting his spirit in order, making it healthier. Writing poems may reflect a similar feeling.

The friendship and correspondence between Benjamin Rush and Thomas Jefferson continued throughout the years from the time when they first met, in 1775, albeit intermittently during extraordinary times. Rush continued working at the Mint during Jefferson's presidency and was in general agreement politically with Jefferson more often than he was with Adams during those years. Adams was aware of this, and of Rush's participation in the Jeffersonian party because Rush was very candid in his letters to Adams. Among the reasons for the solid relationship between Rush and Jefferson was that they were intellectual peers in the company of many brilliant minds—men and women of exceptional, purpose-driven determination. But Jefferson and Rush had more in common than most. Among their shared interests were moral, religious, and philosophical theses—and their practical applications—to governing, foreign relations, public and higher education, anthropology, religion, and the sciences, particularly agriculture and botany, man-made physical structures and architecture, and more. Both were interested in a work published by Erasmus Darwin in 1789, *The Botanic Garden*, which included an article, "Loves of the Plants," in which Darwin deciphered the generation of plants in much the same way that his famous grandson, Charles Darwin, would later study the evolution of man.

The Embargo Act of 1807 was Jefferson's hopeful substitute for becoming caught up in the war between England and France. Both countries refused to recognize an American right to trade as a neutral stance with their enemies. The act cut off overland and inland waterway trade with Canada, prohibited American ships from trading with European nations, and protected American merchant ships from them. "Historians are generally agreed that, though a noble experiment in intention, it was a blunder as practiced."[54] The difficulties faced by Americans during the enforcement of Jefferson's Embargo Act made their way into one of Rush's dreams.

I dreamed that I had been elected President of the United States. At first I objected to accepting the high and honorable station, but upon recollecting that it would give me an opportunity of

exercising my long-cherished hostility to ardent spirits [alcohol]
by putting an end to their general use in our country,
I consented ... and a law was obtained for those purposes.[55]

The dream continued to detail the crisis that followed, between the Empire of Habit, which was imaged as drunkenness, and the Empire of Reason, which was imaged as a goddess. Speaking with an old man who came to protest the law, the "president" told him that the people should submit to the Empire of Reason. The old man responded that "men are rational, not reasonable creatures." He asserted that "one might as well arrest the orbs of heaven in their course as ... change the habits of a whole people." He told the president that "the spirit law was a blunder."[56]

The marriage of "cherished" with "hostility" in the dream about his plan for a sober community doomed the dream ego's presidency: it is another variation on the problem of containing the opposites in a unified whole. In the dream the goddess Reason ruled in the form of president. The people represented a whole cast of Rush's own dissenting views—at odds with himself—about the psychological, physical, and moral consequences of a spirit law. Reason is generally characterized as masculine. Rush, however, cast it in the feminine, thereby mitigating Reason's harsh cutting edge.

This dream ended with an understanding that Reason would not be able to unite the opposites. This was clearly illustrated in Adams's animatical dream as well. Rush awakened grateful to the old man in the dream. He learned from this dream that there were more things inherent in human nature that present themselves through the irrational (as in dreams) than he had known existed or had such power. Rush's mind opened just a bit more to the greater meaning inherent in what he called the irrational.

There was another disjoint in Rush's psyche on the literal topic of alcoholism as a problem in America: he believed that "ardent spirits" when taken into the body, in addition to being unhealthful, acted as irreligious spirits. They quelled inhibitions, created moral lapses, and in consequence put people out of relationship with the better, healing spirits of their religion. He wrote to Adams,

> *I believe [with Jefferson] the Embargo to be a wise, a just, and*
> *a necessary measure, and I believe simple water, molasses...*
> *and small beer to be the best ordinary drinks in the world; but if*
> *mankind will prefer a monarchy to a republic, commerce and war*
> *to an embargo, and drams, slings, grog, and toddy to the wholesome*
> *liquors above-mentioned, I can only testify my sorrow.*[57]

Rush enclosed, with the dream, the new edition of his *Lectures upon Animal Life*. Adams responded,

> *You have more wit and humor and sense in your sleep than*
> *other people, I was about to say, than you have yourself when*
> *awake.... If I could lay an embargo or pass a non-importation*
> *law against corruption and foreign influences, I would not make*
> *it a temporal but a perpetual law, and I would not repeal it,*
> *though it should raise a clamor as loud as my gag law or your*
> *grog law or Mr. Jefferson's Embargo.*[58]

Adams believed the Embargo Act would have consequences similar to those in the dream. He may have identified with the turmoil of Rush's dream ego's presidency—reminding him of the debacle created by his own ill-fated Alien and Sedition Acts during his administration. Adams was upset with Rush for his position on the embargo, and for not having spoken out against it when he had had many opportunities to do so at the debates in Philadelphia and Washington. It is likely that Adams's frustration came in part from his own lack of a platform from which to make his objections known.

Usually entertained by Rush's dreams, though not so this time, Adams rarely understood the dreams as pointing to Rush's internal process but responded mostly to what they might say about external matters. As a consequence he believed that Rush should seek solutions in the outer world that addressed the greater good in the long term rather than what he perceived as selfish expedients that satisfied Rush's personally cherished hostilities (for example, against alcohol). Adams knew Rush better than to think of him as either selfless or selfish. But he did not recognize the significance of the dream as signaling new potential, or alteration, or perhaps the waning spirit of an old attitude currently in the process of dying so that something new could take its place. The dream depicted attitudes whose time was ripe for confrontation. The archetypal schema enacted in the dream embodied the conflicts between Reason and Habit, between collective and individual values and purposes.

More than a century later, Carl Jung reflected on the considerable task of rising above our harassed and perplexed minds in order to animate and relate to resources in the unconscious mind:

> I have devoted considerable space to my subjective view of the
> world, which,…is not a product of rational thinking. It is rather a
> vision such as will come to one who undertakes, deliberately, with
> half-closed eyes and somewhat closed ears, to see and hear
> the form and voice of being. If our impressions are too distinct,
> we are held to the hour and minute of the present and have
> no way of knowing how our ancestral psyches listen to and
> understand the present—in other words, how our unconscious
> is responding to it. Thus we remain ignorant of whether our
> ancestral components find an elementary gratification in our
> lives, or whether they are repelled. Inner peace and contentment
> depend in large measure upon whether or not the historical

CHAPTER FIVE

family which is inherent in the individual can be harmonized with the ephemeral conditions of the present.[59]

Jefferson called upon Rush for medical advice, and their correspondence includes other personal or family-related confidences from time to time. Generally their letters did not have the informal intimacy, personal revelation, artistic style, literary references, and occasional poetic modulations that characterized Rush's and Adams's letters. Instead, Rush and Jefferson developed an intellectual comfort zone in their letters, in which each appears to have enjoyed expressing strongly held opinions that sometimes seemed directed at eliciting highly charged responses—particularly Rush, who was known to be a little indiscreet when writing about other politicians or political ideas, although he always maintained respect for Adams. But while Jefferson and Rush fashioned a more distant intellectual and somewhat formal relationship, they never really injured one another personally with their opinions. On the other hand, Mrs. Adams's letters to Jefferson were known to have hurt Jefferson's feelings. She was particularly sharp with him about his having removed her son, John Quincy Adams, from his government job and replacing him with someone from his own party.[60]

In his less important relationships (as distinguished from Jefferson, Adams, and his family), Rush's feelings were easily wounded. When he met opposition in the course of everyday life, in either of his occupations, political or medical, his temper flared and his mind seemed quite closed to reason or opinions other than his own. Everyday incidents of opposition seemed to pick at old scars and draw old offenses forward, undifferentiated, to meld into the present brouhaha, making it more important than perhaps the incident deserved. This problem, very likely an unannealed psychological complex, tormented him. It is difficult to sort out whether the inflated offenses were exacerbated by the complex and/or whether he was literally on a different wavelength than most people—so that there could be no real interchange of ideas. Rush was of the same celebrated intellectual caliber as Jefferson, though he lagged behind in finesse.

Rush's difficulties may also relate, in part, to his typology. His careers demanded a highly developed sensation function, that is, a facility with facts and activities based on scientific evidence and information gathered by the senses—then applied in the external world. But his intuition, not his sensation function, was the source of his intellectual inspiration and certainties. Intuition as typology involves a kind of foreknowing that has a numinous quality because it indicates, with an intense sense of certainty, the direction of answers—in much the same way that the magnetic pole indicates where the magnetic field is most intense. One consequence was that neither the intuitive Rush nor the people around him could readily understand how he arrived at his conclusions. Backtracking to fill in the blanks was regrettably irritating to him and was typologically the opposite of the comfortable direction for someone of his nature—though until he achieved professional accolades for his work in medicine, he continued to do so. The remarkable evidence of Rush's ability to access and integrate input from all his typological functions is to found in his many and varied accomplishments.

Gradually, between 1802 and 1805, professional conditions took a turn for the better for Rush because his medical discoveries and improvements in his methods demonstrated their efficacy over time. This brought Rush much needed relief and was accompanied by a general shift in his psyche toward a greater sense of freedom. In a letter to Adams, in addition to thanking him for the job that had sustained him through difficult times, Rush wrote: "It has pleased God to produce a reaction of the public mind towards me…Some of my old patients have returned…and many new ones have been added…. I am enabled not only to live comfortably with

a large family and in an expensive city, but to save something...
Even my pen has lately added to my resources. I am to receive 1000
dollars for the copyright of a new edition of my medical works."[61]
Following this exchange, Rush's letters to Adams always included
terms of affection and appreciation. The relief he felt also appears
to have helped him ease into an expanded circle of people with
whom he corresponded. Free rein reinvigorated his intuition, and
a whole constellation of creative ideas soon brought him national
and international recognition, which he very much enjoyed.
Among his publications during this period was "Inquiry into the
Effects of Ardent Spirits upon the Human Body and Mind." The
topic appears in a series of dreams that followed upon the free-
ing up of Rush's intuition, including the one (documented in a
letter dated 16 September 1808) in which Rush dreamed he was
president and passed a law banning alcohol (see pp. 59–60).

Many of the people with whom he corresponded became the
friends in his old age, and most of them had known Adams from
the early days. There was general agreement among his corre-
spondents that while there was still time they wanted Adams and
Jefferson to reconnect with one another and gather their recol-
lections for history and posterity. It was common knowledge that
Europe was storm-driven and that its effect had already reached
American waters and shores. Adams's and Jefferson's friends
believed that those leaders who had learned by experience, who
had created and saved the nation, could teach by example if they
joined together to help in the current crises.

Rush began the effort by encouraging Adams and Jefferson to
set aside their personal feelings in order to model a conciliatory
relationship for the bitterly feuding political parties that were so
set against one another that their focus was distracted from the
dangers looming abroad. In an about-face, made possible by the
easing of strain on him, it became Rush's turn to cajole Adams
into action for the sake of the country. Rush wrote: "If we fly from

the lion of despotism, the bear of anarchy meets us, or if we retire from both and lean our hand upon the wall of our domestic sanctuary, the recollection of past or the dread of future evils bites us like a serpent."[62] Washington was dead. Adams and Jefferson still lived—the pressure to encourage them to communicate with one another came from many directions.

Because we have access to her letters, Abigail Adams, whose life story is emblematic of the heroic women of early America, has transcended her living present in a *coniunctio* with generations to come.[63] Her story is among the "hard won, permanent possessions of humanity."[64] She was aware of her place in history, particularly while she was first lady. But she was more keenly aware of the historic importance of her husband than of herself, and she shared Rush's long view of Adams's place in the lineage of presidents of the United States. Abigail Adams did not wait for her husband to signal his readiness to reconnect with Jefferson. She was a woman of depth who wielded her personal authority with independence and confidence. Those who read what she wrote during those difficult times will find that her life story is an encyclopedia of admirable humanity. Thomas Jefferson would soon find himself answering to her.

They had known one another since before the Revolution, and Abigail knew Jefferson's family well. His wife Martha, apparently a well-liked but frail and sickly woman, died in 1782 of complications from childbirth. Jefferson's eldest daughter, Martha, nicknamed "Patsy," ten years old when her mother died, remained very close to her father throughout his life. She was his hostess when he was president, lived in his house during her marriage, and was nurse to him when he died. But a younger daughter, Maria (often written of as Mary and nicknamed "Polly"), was sent to live with her aunt when her mother died. When Polly was eight years old, Jefferson sent for her to join him in Paris, and on her way there, she lived briefly with Abigail and John Adams, who were representatives living in England at the time. The Adams family was completely enchanted by her, so it is no surprise that Abigail's heart went out to Jefferson when Polly died in 1804. She wrote of her love for Polly and hopes that he might derive comfort and consolation from God, adding that "various reasons had withheld her pen untill the powerfull feelings of my heart, have burst through the restraint and given expression to [my] condolence." Abigail did not resist adding that her letter was from "her who once took pleasure in subscribing Herself your Friend."[65] Jefferson apparently welcomed the renewed correspondence with Abigail, even as he noted the past tense in her letter. There followed a series of letters of surprisingly frank disclosures and discussions of the grievances that had come between them.[66] Abigail did not make this correspondence known to John Adams until the end of 1804. He recorded that he would make no comment on them. For example, Jefferson wrote to Abigail Adams: "One act of Mr. Adams's Life, and one only...ever gave me a moments personal displeasure. I did think his last appointments to office personally unkind. They were from among my most ardent political enemies."[67] Abigail responded that George Washington had filled every appointment before he left office and that Adams had not taken it personally— nor should Jefferson. She wrote that Adams selected persons he felt qualified for the positions. Abigail went on to write, "I have never felt any enmity towards you Sir for being elected president of the United States. But the instruments made use of, and the means which were practised to effect a change, have my utter abhorrence and detestation, for they were the blackest calumny, and foulest falsehoods."[68] Although no reconciliation came of their correspondence for years, neither of them broke the chain of letters or lost the affinity that supported their underlying connection. The relationship grew stronger over time, shedding light on choices, decisions, and feelings in the darkest, usually most guarded, private places in the mind. Throughout the sometimes

exasperated interchange there was no profound feeling of hope-
lessness. The frank, unapologetic, openness of expression in the
correspondence between Abigail Adams and Thomas Jefferson
bore a similarity to that between Adams and Rush. Abigail's correspondence with Jefferson was kept quite apart from her husband's
sphere of activities, interests, and contacts. When he became aware
of the correspondence, Adams intelligently made no objection,
but he declined to read the letters. On the one hand, Adams was
respectful of Abigail, and on the other, he was canny—and perhaps shrewd—in letting the plot develop without his having to
make any concessions or job of it.

Years had passed since the Revolutionary War, but there was no
peace in the world among European nations, which continued to
harangue one another. In America, meanwhile, the Constitution
had been written. Washington, Adams, and then Jefferson did
their best to apply its designer configuration to the unfolding
of democracy during their terms in office, and then went home.
Benjamin Rush also went home.

chapter six

Benjamin Rush's Prophetic Dream

Rush felt that he had one remaining, compelling, moral obligation in service to his country, and that was to induce Adams and
Jefferson to reestablish the friendship that had fallen away when
Adams lost his second term to Jefferson. The two embodied opposites in many opinions, and it seemed to Rush that it should all be
revealed—that they must reconcile so that they could tell the story
of America in the first person for the generations to come.

Eight years to the day had passed since Adams had left the
White House. He wrote to Rush: "Jefferson expired and Madison
came to Life, last night at twelve o'clock....I pity poor Madison.
Will you be so good as to take a Nap, and dream for my Instruction
and edification a Character of Jefferson and His Administration?"[69]
Rush did dream, and then he sent the dream to Adams.

My dear friend,
What would [you] think of some future historian of the
United States concluding one of his chapters with the following
(my dream)...
   "What book is that in your hands?" said I to my son Richard
a few nights ago in a DREAM? "It is the history of the United
States," said he. "Shall I read a page of it to you?" "No, no,"
said I....."But sir," said my son, "this page relates to your friend
Mr. Adams." "Let me see it then," said I.

1809

*Among the most extraordinary events of this year was the
renewal of the friendship and intercourse between Mr. John
Adams and Mr. Jefferson, the two ex-Presidents of the United
States. They met for the first time in Congress in 1775. Their
principles of liberty, their ardent attachment to their country, and
their views of the importance and probable issue of the struggle
with Great Britain in which they were engaged being exactly
the same, they were strongly attracted to each other and became
personal as well as political friends. They met in England during
the war while each of them held commissions of honor and trust
at two of the first courts of Europe, and spent many happy hours
together in reviewing the difficulties and success of their respective
negotiations. A difference of opinion upon the objects and issue of
the French Revolution separated them during the years in which
that great event interested and divided the American people. The
predominance of the party which favored the French cause threw
Adams out of the Chair of the United States in the year 1800
and placed Mr. Jefferson there in his stead. The former retired
with resignation and dignity to his seat at Quincy, where he
spent the evening of his life in literary and philosophical pursuits
surrounded by an amiable family and a few old and affectionate
friends. The latter resigned the Chair of the United States in
the year 1808, sick of the cares and disgusted with the intrigues
of public life, and retired to his seat at Monticello in Virginia,
where he spent the remainder of his days in the cultivation of
a large farm agreeably to the new system of husbandry. In the
month of November 1809, Mr. Adams addressed a short letter to
his friend Mr. Jefferson in which he congratulated him upon his
escape to the shades of retirement and domestic happiness, and
concluded it with assurances of his regard and good wishes for his
welfare. This letter did great honor to Mr. Adams. It discovered
a magnanimity known only to great minds. Mr. Jefferson*

replied to this letter and reciprocated expressions of regard and
esteem. These letters were followed by a correspondence of several
years, in which they mutually reviewed the scenes of business
in which they had been engaged, and candidly acknowledged to
each other all the errors of opinion and conduct into which they
had fallen during the time they filled the same station in the
service of their country. Many a precious aphorisms, the result
of observation, experience, and profound reflection, it is said,
are contained in these letters. It is to be hoped the world will be
favored with a sight of them when they can neither injure nor
displease any persons or families whose ancestors' follies or crimes
were mentioned in them. These gentlemen sunk into the grave
nearly at the same time, full of years, and rich in the gratitude
and praises of their country (for they outlived the heterogeneous
parties that were opposed to them), and to their numerous merits
and honors posterity has added that they were rival friends."[70]

Rush had had this prophetic dream in October 1809, four years
prior to his own death and seventeen years before Adams and
Jefferson both died on 4 July 1826.

Adams replied, "A DREAM AGAIN! I wish you would dream
all day and all night, for one of your dreams puts me in spirits for
a month. I have no other objection to your dream but that it is not
history. It may be prophecy."[71]

In his study of dreams throughout the years, Rush's idea of
them as a version of madness, because they are evidence of the
irrational in the human mind, evolved. His thought that they
must be "cured" fell away, though his idea of writing them down
remained constant. Rush responded to Adams and enclosed his
book describing the new generation of his theory on dreams:

[T]his faculty has not yet found its way into our systems of
physiology.... I mean... that principle [dreaming] is as much a

native faculty as memory or imagination…. [It is] a source of knowledge, so necessary to individual comfort and social existence [that] has not been made dependent upon our senses, nor left to the slow inductions of reason.[72]

With regard to prophetic dreams, von Franz wrote:

> In our conscious lives events sometimes seem new or sudden, whereas in the unconscious they have a long previous history. Prophetic dreams represent the inclination of the psyche to move forward toward the future in advance of consciousness. Prophetic dreams are difficult to understand because their meaning is only realized at a future time.[73]

Jung referred to the intersection of the unconscious prophecy with an outer event of identical meaning as "synchronistic phenomena." He wrote that the relation between the unconscious and matter remains as yet an unfathomed secret.

Over the next two years, Rush pumped up his efforts to reconcile Adams and Jefferson with an urgent, sympathetic, dramatic appeal to their patriotism and sense of posterity. He assured both Jefferson and Adams that human nature would "be the gainer by it."[74] Then in a letter to Adams he wrote, "The time cannot be very distant when you and I must both sleep with our fathers."[75] His letter contained a panegyric of Adams's character and accomplishments, and he requested that Adams compose a "posthumous address to the citizens of the United States."[76] Adams responded, "Your letter of the 20th… filled my eyes with tears and, indurate stoic as I am, my heart with sensations unutterable by my tongue or pen."[77] Adams went on to enumerate fifteen reasons why he should and would not comply. Rush wrote back that he did not agree with any of Adams's reasons and insisted that "no hand but your own must compose your voice from the tomb."[78] This ball was tossed back and forth across the court until Rush finally confessed:

> *Mr. Jefferson and I exchanged letters once in six, nine, or twelve months. This day I received a few lines from him in which he introduces your name in the following words. [Rush quoting Jefferson:] "Among other things he [Mr. Adams] averted to the unprincipled licentiousness of the press against myself.... There is an awkwardness which hangs over the resuming a correspondence so long discontinued unless something should arise which should call for a letter. Time and chance may perhaps generate such an occasion, of which I shall not be wanting in promptitude to avail myself."[79]*

Adams wrote that he was at a loss how to answer the letter and added:

> *I perceive plainly enough, Rush, that you have been teasing Jefferson to write to me, as you did me some time ago to write to him.... You often put me in mind that I am soon to die; I know it and shall not forget it.... But why do you make so much ado about nothing? Of what use can it be for Jefferson and me to exchange letters? I have nothing to say to him but to wish him an easy journey to heaven when he goes, which I wish may be delayed as long as life shall be agreeable to him. And he can have nothing to say to me but to bid me make haste and be ready. Time and Chance, however, or possibly design, may produce ere long a letter between us."[80]*

chapter seven

John Adams's Theater Dream: A Play Within a Dream

The correspondence between Rush and Adams settled in to a friendly exchange about everyday matters and people they had in common. Rush wrote: "You have so far outdreamed me in your last letter that I shall be afraid hereafter to let my imagination loose in that mode of exposing my folly and vice."[81] He went on to describe his visit to another old Revolutionary friend. "I am now visiting Mr. Clymer, who is indisposed. I read your [Versailles] dream to him yesterday. [He said:] 'What an imagination the old gentleman possesses!'"[82] Adams responded to Rush's letter with a little story about his day out for a ride on Hobby.

Dear Rush,

One day after a long ride upon Hobby I came home well exercised, in good health and spirits, went to bed, to sleep, and dreamed. I shall not give you the dramatic persons at length.... I shall only give you a hint of a part of one scene.

An open theater was erected in the center of a vast plain in Virginia, where were assembled all the inhabitants of U.S., eight millions of people, to see a new play, advertised as the most extraordinary that ever was represented on any stage, excelling Menander, Terence, Shakespeare, Corneille, and Molière.

FIG. 9 Captain Isaac Hull, USN. Photograph of an oil painting by Gilbert Stuart. U.S. Naval Historical Center, Washington, D.C. The original is hung in the Boston Museum of Fine Arts. The vignette below the painting is an original sketch made under the direction of Capt. Hull.

FIG. 10 Captain Jacob Jones, USN. From a crayon portrait by Albert Rosenthal after a painting by Rembrandt Peale. U.S. Naval Historical Center, Washington, D.C.

A distant view of the ocean was presented with Hull and his Constitution, *blazing away his horizontal volcano of a broadside at the* Guerriere, *which is soon seen to explode; after the explosion, the* Constitution *sails majestically but slowly along the whole length of the theater and comes to anchor, in full sight of the audience; then Jones with his* Frolic *succeeded an anchored near the* Constitution, *and it was remarkable that the audience applauded him with as much enthusiasm as Hull.*[83] *... After a pause for the spectators to gaze and admire, Mrs. Siddons was selected to address the audience.*[84] *Slowly and gracefully swimming over the stage, she approached near enough to be heard by all, with all the advantages of her face, figure, gestures, and intonations, pointing with her hand to the glorious spectacle of the navy, in the words of Adam to Eve when she first saw her face in the clear stream, she only said,*

"America! This, fair Creature, is thyself!

"Sampson! There, is thy Lock of divine Power!

"Hercules! Behold the emblem of thy Strength (which) is to subdue Monsters and conquer Oppressors.

"David! Lo, thy sling, which is to bring Goliath to Reason!"[85] *Observing that this overgrown colt of a nation had, after all this, no feeling of its strength nor any sense of its glory, any more than my Hobby, I obtained a speaking trumpet and made a motion, which was carried, that the play should be dismissed and the nation resolve itself into a committee of the whole house on the state of the nation, Dr. Rush in the chair. It was my intention to record the phizzes of the tories, about one third; the speeches of the deep Democrats, about another third, who abused me so much a dozen or fourteen years ago on account of my navy, which is now saving them from destruction.*

The exultations of the remaining third, who had been always friendly to naval defense, which ... amounted to little more than "Did we not always tell you so?"

*The sensations and reflection of Jefferson, Madison, Giles, &c.,
as well as their oration, you may imagine....*

*The vote was called and a small majority heavily and
languidly appeared for a few 74 and twenty frigates.*

*Oh! The wisdom! The foresight and hindsight, the rightsight
and the leftsight, the northsight and the southsight, the eastsight
and the westsight, that appeared in the august assembly! Many
Quaker women, Dr. Dwight, and Dr. Osgood spoke, and had
Joel (Barlow) been there, no doubt he would have delivered an
epic poem.*

*So such business could not be done in a short time. The sun
now blazed through the windows upon my eyes and awoke me.*[86]

FIG. 11 Capture of the H.B.M. Sloop of War *Frolic,* Captain Whinyates, by
the U.S. Sloop of War *Wasp,* Captain Jacob Jones, after a close action of 43
minutes, October 18, 1812. Aquatint in colors, drawn and engraved by F. Kearny
from a sketch by Lieut. Claxton of the *Wasp.* Courtesy of Beverley R. Robinson
Collection, U.S. Naval Academy.

This is the second of the only two dreams known to have survived that Adams recorded and shared with Rush. In a happy synchronicity, it brings a measure of circularity to Adams's story in that it recalls the earlier dream (of 1790), while at the same time providing an updated version that helps to account for much that happened in between.

The format of the dream echoes the architecture of his earlier dream, thereby highlighting the changes in the themes that developed over time.

1790	1812
lofty scaffold	theater erected
center of great plain	center of vast plain
in Versailles	in Virginia
innumerable congregation	all the inhabitants
25 million	8 million
royal menagerie	people
active persuasion	passive, see a play
as good as all rhetoricians	better than Shakespeare, etc.
anarchic animals (innumerable)	Hobby (the "one")
caught in the fray	observing the fray
defeat	success
distaste and regression	applause and integration

Each step along the progression brought Adams closer to home, more in touch with people, less responsible for the pursuit of national interests but no less interested in them. The unconscious progression was from identification with an idea of nationhood to identification with the realized nation, from leadership to membership, and from anxiety to calm to fulfillment.

A play within a dream offers unusual opportunities for symbolic expression. Ideas are attached to the archetype of theater that shape and participate in its meaning, among them the architecture

FIG. 12 *Sarah Siddons as "Tragic Muse"* (1787). Engraving by Francis Haward after portrait by Sir Joshua Reynolds. National Portrait Gallery, London.

itself, the anticipation of visual expression off and on the stage, and the actors. Importantly, since the actors can only say or do what is written for them, they are couriers for expressions from the creator. In an analytic approach to Adams's dream play, the playwright or creative source is considered to be the Self.

Of the many symbolic representations in the dream, four in particular reveal its essential message:

The scaffold and its stage, and the theater and its stage
Mrs. Siddons as the artful anima
Adams's Eve, the new beginning
Adam in Adams's dream

An ambiguous archetypal symbol, the scaffold is the ticking clock of contending opposites. One meaning of the word *scaffold* is constructive; it may serve, temporarily, to support the development or extend the life of a structure forward in time The opposite of that idea is more like the one in Adams's dream. This version of *scaffold*, as associated with Versailles, is notorious for its trapdoor and guillotine—danger hovering above and below—lofty to enhance the viewing experience of capital punishment fans and to provide a platform perhaps for a few last words. Its structural purpose is to keep the speeches really short and terminate the life lived ever so briefly on its staging boards. It was from a site such as this, in his annimatical dream, that Adams's dream ego made its narrow escape. Three years after he recalled the dream and sent it to Rush, the French king and Marie Antoinette were guillotined at Versailles.

The theater and its stage constitute a new generation of the elevated platform that in the earlier dream was a lofty scaffold. This makes the stage in the dream of 1812 an imagination-evoking symbol, one more akin to the empty page of an open book. It invites lives to be lived or forfeited upon it. The stage itself has an imagination: on its horizontal plane it can contain, in seamless harmony, vistas as limitless as oceans or as small and intimate as an overheard interior sigh. Of its vertical imagination it can be said that the stage extends itself within itself so that the mind accepts that trapdoors may lead down into the lower reaches of the author's or dreamer's mind—or extend up to the heavenly legends and beyond. Backstage imitates the unconscious or the shadow and the lurking unseen, unknown aspects of the psyche. The stage makes possible every point of view that might be needed to deliver a unit of expression: northsight, southsight, rightsight and so on. The tension at the crux of the horizontal and vertical architecture of the psyche's internal stage gives rise to the soliloquy of the mind.

The theater and its stage is a likeness to the collective unconscious. In a sleeping state, in a likeness of perfect privacy, the symbols express themselves and speak the inner Self into being.

The first scene in the play is a distant view of the ocean with Adams's dream navy blasting canons like volcanoes and exploding British ships. Then, like great matadors who turn their backs to the defeated bull and parade themselves around the arena, America's signature naval heroes reset their sails, turn their backs on the defeated British, and sail slowly along the length of the theater in full sight of an admiring audience. It is a glorious display of the paradoxical masculine: power and Eros are the necessities in warriors for peacekeeping.

Mrs. Siddons played the counterpart to the masculine elements in the war scene, giving a dramatic performance of enigmatic connotation. The most famous British actress of the time, her watery presence downstage in the spectacle of warring battleships upstage seemed odd in many ways. Then I imagined Marie-Louise von Franz witnessing such a sight. It would have been like her to exclaim, "Who would be swimming prettily in the sea where a battle is taking place? What is this anima up to?" Her question sent me searching for an answer. For me, born in Boston, the scene hearkened back in time to the British and the Boston Tea Party. Spoon-fed stories that burbled up from Boston Harbor when I was a child, I developed a love of country along with a sense of borrowed pride and power. For this quest to find an answer to von Franz's question, I imagined borrowing garments and costuming myself with deceit as Siddons had done in the dream and as the colonists had done at the Tea Party. I helped toss the tea into the harbor, upending and undoing the ruling principles, and threw off the scent of my intent. I was, for that single moment, like a new nation being formed. I dressed the actress Mrs. Siddons in the notorious Stamp Act–stamped costume—a crate of British tea. She dips and smiles, seeming like the times—all

FIG. 13 *Sarah Siddons* (1793), shown at a monument to Shakespeare in her role as Lady Macbeth. Portrait by Sir William Beechey. National Portrait Gallery, London.

the while unknowingly altering the harbor water—preparing it to swallow British ships. In my borrowed garments it is easier for me to recognize her among the other players. Then I began to find the answer to von Franz's question.

Mrs. Siddons was best known to Adams during his time as ambassador to England, for her part as Lady Macbeth in Shakespeare's *Macbeth*. Her identification with the part begs the question of whether Mrs. Siddons was authentic in her praises or was an artfully painted actress on Adams's dream stage, seeming to admire the defeat of the navy of her own country.

As a dream figure, removed from consciousness by sleep and more deeply removed by the immersion in water, Mrs. Siddons underscored her proclamations by calling out names that would validate her praises. She likened Hull and Jones to Sampson, Hercules, and David, three mythic heroes who were all brought down by women of tribes or cultures other than their own. Her heroes' stories conclude with the failed marriage between power and Eros. In Siddons's part in *Macbeth*, due to her will to power, Lady Macbeth undergoes a decline as an anima figure. She descends from her role as Eros partner to Macbeth to a state in which she willfully destroys the feminine qualities essential to Eros. Having killed the better side of herself as anima, she sleep-walks through disintegration to her baffled death. Lady Macbeth successfully evoked Macbeth's inferior shadow masculine quali-ties. Where he had been valiant, loyal, and heroic, he became self-centered, ambitious, traitorous, and uncaring. Having been seduced into relationship with the transformed dark side of the anima, he eventually followed her, deluded and defiant to his death.

The next generation of the feminine to supplant Mrs. Siddons in the dream was the first biblical woman in the generations of women, Eve. In Adams's dream, prior to her praise of the heroes, it was said that Mrs. Siddons was speaking the lines Adam had spoken to Eve when she first saw her face in a clear stream. Eve's reflection in clear water speaks of a new development in consciousness. The dream personification acts as a reminder that Eve, who was a development in Adam, would be a new version of anima.[87] With Mrs. Siddons in the dream, one never really knew what she portended—she was best known for her "seeming." Opposites in the feminine were raised in the shape of Eve in the dream, to end an age of innocence on the eve of a great change in Adams's psyche.

Mrs. Siddons also introduced double entendre into the masculine figure in the dream, Adam in Adams's dream. The literal biblical commentary on Eve has been that she was a development out of Adam, rather than in Adam. But the psychological event of Eve in Adams's dream describes the revised version of Adam and Adams's anima: representing a unity in the "one." For John Adams this dream brought momentous spiritual renewal. A great psychological largess flowed into Adams's psyche and led to his decision, in the dream, to dismiss the play.

What followed was Adams's ascent from the depth of sleep through the dissipating veil of unconsciousness. A second curtain parted to show him a different reality. Speeches were spoken by people he knew, representing the various points of view usually expressed in Adams's waking life. Wholeness revealed itself in his exclamation about wisdom, "Oh! The wisdom! The foresight and hindsight, ..."—all the elements of a structural mandala. The dismissal of the play implies that the distance, and impersonal point of view, provided to an observer at the theater was no longer needed. That part, the play, had served its purpose.

As had happened with Rush and Descartes, the dream moved Adams to a place where he would have liked to go voluntarily, but in the past he had succumbed to qualms that were very strong against it. The consummate founding father, his compass had cycled through a collective structural mandala, dreaming the dream for all Americans—*entre nous fabula narratur.* But the spirit of the times, which calls human beings into their own personal lives, *de te fabula narratur,* requires that one be centered on one's own axis. This image reflects the inclination of human beings toward new ideas and inspirations often not yet known in waking life. It remained for Adams's dreaming mind to point the way to reconcile the two forces that pulled at him, within him. The problem of reconciling them required the development of a third, or new, generation of comprehensive inclusiveness. Out of Adam(s) had to come a new Adam(s) and a revised anima, Eve. But *vir unis* was only one step on Adams's path to individuation. The next would require equinity. He came upon it, synchronistically, along a path in the forest.

Hobby/Chiron

Synchronicity is an acausal connecting principle—meaning that the cause of the intersection cannot be understood or explained by rational methodologies. Rather, it is an example of the irrational at work as a nonlinear, source-motivated functional link. Synchronicities such as Adams's encounter with the man and the horse have a fairy-tale quality to them. It is as if Adams had been guided by an unconscious hunch to the place where he would meet the man and his horse. Adams enclosed the story of his encounter in the envelope with the dream in his letter to Rush. Here is an abbreviated version:

> *On horseback on my way to Weymouth on a visit to my friend Dr. Tufts, I met a man leading a horse, who asked if I wanted to buy... a colt of three years old that month of November, his sucking teeth were not shed, he was 17 or 18 hands high, bones like massy timber, ribbed quite to his hips, every way broad, strong, and well filled in proportion, as tame, gentle, good-natured and good-humored as a cosset lamb. Thinks I to myself, this noble creature is the exact emblem of my dear country. I will have him and call him my Hobby. He may carry me five and twenty or 30 years if I should live. I [will] ride him every day when the weather suits, but I should shudder if he should ever discover or feel his own power. By one vigorous exertion of his strength, he*

might shake me to the ground, on the right hand or the left, pitch
me over his head, or throw me back over his rump.[88]

The directions in which Adams could be pitched are counterpart
on the physical level to the foresight, hindsight, rightsight, leftsight in the accompanying dream.

Animals generally represent physical and instinctual forces
in the dreamer and bring their unique characteristics to describe
a condition in the unconscious. In the earlier dream the menagerie was a disunity of elements; in Hobby, we see a unity of "one."
Adams's meeting with Hobby is his story of the hard psychological work in service of individuation. Its emblem is the Self figure,
Hobby. The partnership of man and horse is a partnership of ego
with animal spirit. The ego directs the horse and the animal spirit
provides power and life. It is deeply relieving when the aging ego
feels it can let free the rein, knowing that one's own equinity will
find the way home. The archetypal image of horse-and-rider
combined as a team has its roots in the mythical figure Chiron.

Adams's journey to the meeting likely began twenty years
earlier with the first dream, which left open the question of
whether his relationship with the anarchic menagerie would trans-
form over time. Hobby represented the answer; the meeting in the
forest was a meeting in the mind.

Rush wrote,

I was much gratified with your account of your conversations at
two... public dinners. But I was more struck with the wonderful
health and spirits which you discover in being able at 77 to occupy
a chair at a large convivial [gathering]... and afterwards ride 12
miles in the dark or by moonlight to Quincy.[89]

Adams replied, "If you would have an old man or an old horse good for anything, you must keep him always going, always in use."[90] Rush also wrote a letter directed to Hobby himself.

I hasten… to pay my respects… Mr. Hobby. Treat gently and safely, highly favored beast, while your master bestrides your back. Shake every blood vessel of his body, and gently agitate every portion of his brain. Keep up the circulation of his blood for years to come, and excite aphorisms and anecdotes and dreams for the instruction and amusement of his friends by the action of his brain upon his mind.[91]

Hobby "wrote" to Rush:

Honored and Learned Sir,
Be pleased to accept my humble duty for the notice you have condescended to take of me. I will do my best to shake a little animation into my master for a few days or months or possibly years.[92]

FIG. 14 *Chiron* (1973). Drawing by Carrie Judem.

The bulk of Hobby's letter is very puzzling. There are two pages of peculiar, often incorrect, arithmetical calculations. They appear to represent an effort to reconcile Hobby's concern about Adams's well-being by means of a mathematical formula. In one of the calculations, Hobby added to 77 (Adams's age) to the number of years Adams had spent in an occupation. For example, Hobby writes, "Adams is 77. He spent 8 years as Vice-President. These 8 went away like a nauseous fog. Add such 8 to his age, and you make him 85."[93] In others of his calculations, the number or cluster of years Hobby added to 77 is not related to occupation or to content. For example, Hobby writes, "He is 77 and more; 3 and 20 years will make him 100; 13 years will make him 90."[94] Hobby closes his peculiar litany to Rush with a very feeling sentence: "Oh! I have some scruples of conscience, whether I ought to preserve him... Remember... it is a Horse that asks the question."[95]

In Hobby's letter the numbers themselves have no logical meaning, they are there to convey a meaningful feeling. The earlier innumerable menagerie that was not to be counted was also a use of numbers to produce a valence or impression. In both dreams, and in general, numbers are archetypes. Even empty of the properties and objects of meaning, numbers bring order into the chaos of appearances.[96] Numbers create an aura of mystery and numinosity, which, when combined with the feeling-filled comments that accompany them, bring a higher order. In both dreams they rise to consciousness bringing pressure to bear upon moral considerations. In the annimatical dream the moral question relates to ruling principles. In the Hobby letter the moral concern is its reverse—this time, the animal considers the welfare of the man. Hobby writes, "I have some scruples of conscience...."[97]

The descent into feeling that came out of the theater dream and the Hobby letter moved Adams into a happy, productive period in his old age.

CHAPTER EIGHT

Thomas Jefferson

In another synchronous event that intersected at this juncture in time, Rush's efforts to reconcile Adams and Jefferson began to bear fruit. Visitors to Adams, the Cole brothers, one of whom was secretary to President Madison, also visited Jefferson. They told Jefferson that in talking about the early years with Adams, he exclaimed that he had always loved Jefferson, and still loved him. Jefferson told them that this was enough for him and wrote to Rush, "I only needed this knowledge to revive towards him all the affections of the most cordial moments of our lives."[98]

Rush jumped at this chance, encouraging both to embrace the opportunity. On New Years Day, 1812, Adams sent Jefferson two pieces of homespun cloth, along with expressions of respect and wishes for a Happy New Year. Three weeks later Jefferson answered.

> *I thank you...A letter from you calls up recollections very dear to my mind. It carries me back to the times when, beset with difficulties and dangers, we were fellow laborers in the same cause... Laboring always at the same oar, with some wave ever ahead threatening to overwhelm us and yet passing harmless under our bark, we knew not how, we rode through the storm with heart and hand, and made a happy port.... I have given up [politics and] newspapers in exchange for Tacitus and Thucydides,*

for Newton and Euclid; and I find myself much the happier...
I am on horseback 3. or 4. hours of every day; visit 3. or 4. times
a year a [second house] 90 miles distant, performing the winter
journey on horseback. I walk little however; a single mile being
too much for me; and I live in the midst of my grandchildren,
one of whom has lately promoted me to be a great grandfather.
I have heard with pleasure that [your days are similar to mine].
I should have the pleasure of knowing that, in the race of life, you
do not keep, in it's physical decline, the same distance ahead of me
which you have done in political honors and achievements. No
circumstances have lessened the interest I feel in these particulars
respecting yourself; none have suspended for one moment my
sincere esteem for you; and I now salute you with unchanged
affections and respect. [99]

The letters quickly became the happy centerpiece of Adams's waking thoughts and activity. Theirs became the partnership Rush had hoped for. His prophetic dream of 6 September 1809 was midway to its incarnation with the resumption of their friendship; the remainder of its prediction lay fourteen years into the future.

Adams's play within a dream came near the end of the first year of Adams's and Jefferson's renewed correspondence. Abigail Adams passed away during its second year. Adams wrote to Jefferson,

Now sir, for my Griefs! The dear Partner of my Life for fifty four
Years as a Wife and for many Years more as a Lover, now lyes
in extremis, forbidden to speak or be spoken to. If human Life is
a Bubble, no matter how soon it breaks. If it is as I firmly believe
an immortal Existence We ought patiently to wait the
Instructions of the great Teacher. I am, sir, your deeply afflicted
Friend John Adams. [100]

In the third year Benjamin Rush wrote his final letter to Adams:

> *I rejoice with you in the 5th naval victory of our country ....*
> *Adieu! my dear old friend... Knowing that my time is short*
> *and that the night of imbecility of mind or of death is fast*
> *approaching, I have sat down to prepare two small tracts...*
> *they relate to the nature of diseases. It will be accommodated*
> *to all classes of readers.*[101]

Adams responded:

> *Dear Rush,... On that subject my feelings are unutterable....*
> *Your time will be well applied in preparing your two tracts*
> *for the press. Posterity will do you justice. "Sons will blush their*
> *fathers were your foes." So wishes and so believes, without a*
> *doubt, one who is and who was and who will be your friend.*
> *John Adams.*[102]

Adams wrote to Julia Rush:

Dear Madam,
Yesterday morning hoping to receive a letter from your husband,
the messenger brought me a letter ... with the melancholy, the
afflicting account of his death. There is not a man ... for whom
I had so tender an affection ... The worth of this dear departed
friend, his talents, his virtues, his services to his country and
to mankind are far beyond my powers to describe. They are
fortunately recorded in his imperishable works .... He has left you,
Madam, for your consolation sons and daughters worthy of him
and of you, ornaments to their family and their country.[103]

Jefferson wrote to Adams: "Another of our friends of 76 is gone, my dear Sir, another of the Co-signers of the independence of our country. And a better man, than Rush, could not have left us, more benevolent, more learned, of finer genius, or more honest."[104] Adams replied to Jefferson: "I know of no Character living or dead, who has done more real good in America than Rush."[105]

Rush's prophetic dream caught up with its gnosis upon the deaths Adams and Jefferson, both on the same day, 4 July 1823:

Dear and Venerable Friend,
... is this the 4th of July? What a group of ideas are associated
with those words! Patriots and heroes rise before me, some
of them just emerging from their graves. They ask the news of
the day ... They inquire into the conduct and characters of the
members of the present Congress ....
Benjn: Rush [106]

Epilogue

Just prior to the October 2009 release of C.G. Jung's Red Book, a *New York Times* newspaper article tucked into its description of the fidgety fears about its potentially great, potentially terrible reception a lovely quote from Jung's advice to a patient of his. It was advice for processing what went on in the deeper and sometimes frightening parts of his patient's mind. The advice has the feel and essential qualities of respect for meaning to be found in the silent sanctuaries of the mind. Jung's Red Book itself was just such a sanctuary for him—as were Rush's and Adams's dreams and discussions written more than two hundred years ago. Jung told his patient:

> I should advise you to put it all down as beautifully as you can—
> in some beautifully bound book. It will seem as if you were making
> the visions banal—but then you need to do that—then you are
> freed from the power of them.…Then when these things are in
> some precious book you can go to the book & turn over the pages
> & for you it will be your church—your cathedral—the silent places
> of your spirit where you will find renewal. If anyone tells you that
> it is morbid or neurotic and you listen to them—then you will lose
> your soul—for the book is your soul.[107]

"THE REMAINDER"

What follows is the dream I had following Adams's prompting at the doorway of my writing room.

*I am walking outside in New England where I grew up—in
a snowy area with myself as a child (age 8), holding her hand.*

In her other hand she is holding a piece of her art—a drawing. The lower section of it, folded so often that it was too weak to hold, blows off in the wind into the snowy street. It is early evening. "Please get me my remainder," she pleads. I bring her to a safe place on the snow-covered lawn, away from the street— then wait for a snowplow, its headlights glowing, to pass along the hard-packed snowy street. I go get her "remainder" and give it into her hand. A sense of contentment settles over us.

I had a relatively unusual version of dyspraxia associated with dyslexia when I was young. My anarchic menagerie of exotic creatures was made up of letters and numbers. I felt their instincts emanating. They were filled with numinous, terrifying import. When letters or numbers came jittering along the chalkboard or a page I got very scared. Sometimes I watched and imagined they were trying to line up and tell me something. But they did not. They were mute. They looked like body parts looking for the other end of themselves. I hoped they would work their way into some sort of picture that I could draw—and that way I would, perhaps, befriend them and remember the word in case it came along again. I had no luck with numbers at all, but over time I sometimes caught the image that letters were trying to form. Then the pictures I drew of them became my most valued possessions. I remember when the *h* in "house" first stood still and looked like a chimney, and the *o* found itself a place as a round window, and the excitement as *u, s,* and *e* simply fell into the picture and formed themselves into a word-picture of a house. As my psyche developed increasing facility with interior, unspoken language, I in turn looked to the image as one would to a spirit guide—to help me understand the world around me. So when in my dream, the little girl called for her "remainder," I knew it was a page in her book to be valued as a conversation with the soul. In the course of my childhood search for a unifying and cooperative relationship with letters and numbers, I came upon that silent sanctuary of living symbols, the image.

Though I befriended my peculiar inspirators, I felt quite alone in the psychic sanctuary until I came upon Mr. Adams's statue some years later. At his feet I studied "silent sanctuaries" with him. Now I know how very fortunate I was to have been tutored by the unuttered influence of the resident archetype at that inelegant statue. At the time of the dream I was working along, writing about John Adams, and concerned that including myself in my book might be narcissistic. But in fact Adams called her up. And then Jung chimed in: "If anyone tells you that it is morbid or neurotic and you listen to them—then you will lose your soul—for the book is your soul."

Everything was a "remainder" to her because nothing fit in— until she discovered the exquisite form. I dedicate this book to the little girl and to the "remainder" as a cherished ideal.

Postscript

Benjamin Rush recognized that the American Revolution was the most important event in modern history. He was very disturbed about the rewriting of history early on in books written second-hand by people who were not there or not central to the creation of the nation. He began his efforts immediately to convince Adams to write his memoirs or a history for the benefit of mankind. Adams tried but found he could not bear the prospect of going through the boxes and stacks of papers he had hauled home from the White House. Many of them are still there in the brick library John Quincy Adams built next door to Adams's house to protect them from fire.

Thomas Jefferson was overjoyed to be finished with his presidency and away from politics. He was a polymath in the world of his other interests and never wrote a history. Much of his original material is valued and curated at the university he founded in Virginia. Were it not for Benjamin Rush, the extraordinary history would not have been written by Adams and Jefferson—we have it now in the form of their historic correspondence. Benjamin Rush's papers, books, and articles are scattered in collections at several universities and historic museums. The Rosenbach Museum in Philadelphia has preserved many of Rush's unpublished dreams and poems. There they await recognition as products of the unconscious that exerted unseen power and influenced the course and recording of history.

FIG. 16 *Gabriel Weather Vane* (1939), by Lucille Chabot. National Gallery of Art, Washington, D.C.

1 Edith Hamilton quoted by David McCullough, *The Course of Human Events*, Jefferson Lecture in the Humanities, Washington, D.C., 2003 (Audioworks, 2005).

2 Letter to Louisa Catherine Adams in L. H. Butterfield, editor, *The Adams Papers: Diary and Autobiography of John Adams* (Cambridge, Mass.: Belknap Press of Harvard University Press, 1962), Diary I, p. xxxv fn.

3 Ibid., Diary I, 24 December 1818.

4 The stone library was designed by Edward Clark Cabot and constructed in 1869–70.

5 *The Adams Papers*, Diary I, 18 January 1847, and J.Q. Adams's will, p. xxvi fn 3. Charles Adams completed quite a bit of the work in his lifetime. The editors of the diaries and autobiography, who picked up where John Quincy and Charles left off, commented, "The Chief deficiencies of the Memoirs are first, that such a very great deal had to be left out, especially relative to Adams' personal as distinct from his public life, in order to compress the text... as the editor and publisher required; and, second, the almost total absence of editorial notes and commentary" (ibid.). Butterfield notes that the personal material, including dreams, was not adequately valued at the time and was edited out, an incalculable loss to psychology and to history.

6 C.G. Jung, "On the Nature of the Psyche" (1954), in *CW*, vol. 8 (Princeton, N.J.: Princeton University Press, 1969), par. 423.

7 Letter from John Adams to Benjamin Rush, 12 April 1809, in John A. Schutz and Douglass Adair, editors, *The Spur of Fame* (Indianapolis: The Liberty Fund, 2001), p. 65.

8 David McCullough, *1776* (New York: Simon and Schuster, 2006), p. 524.

9 Letter from Benjamin Rush to Mr. Bellknap, 13 July 1789, in L.H. Butterfield, ed., *Letters of Benjamin Rush* (Princeton, N.J.: Princeton University Press, 1951), p. 531.

10 Rush's youngest son, William, was born 11 May 1801.

11 In 1799 Benjamin Rush published "Observations upon the Origin of the Malignant Bilious, or Yellow Fever in Philadelphia, and upon the Means of Preventing It" (a pamphlet), and in 1801 he published his *Six Introductory Lectures upon the Institutes and Practice of Medicine* (Philadelphia: Conrad Publishers). See Butterfield, ed., *Letters of Benjamin Rush*, vol. 2, p. 814 fn.

12 Abigail Adams was an extraordinary woman and justice cannot be done her here, except in small part where personally relevant and related to the interpretation of Adams's dreams. The life of Abigail Adams, her ideas,

13 attitudes, relationship with John, and their extensive correspondence are well preserved, documented, and available in many volumes of historic and psychological interest.

13 Stoneyfield came to be known as "Peacefield."

14 Schutz and Adair, eds., *The Spur of Fame*, pp. 4–5.

15 Letter from John Adams to Cotton Tufts, 26 December 1800. Quoted in David McCullough, *John Adams* (New York: Simon and Schuster, 2002), p. 568.

16 Letter dated 8 March 1801, in Lester J. Cappon, editor, *The Adams–Jefferson Letters: The Complete Correspondence Between Thomas Jefferson and Abigail and John Adams* (Chapel Hill: The University of North Carolina Press, 1988), p. 264.

17 Letter from John Adams to Thomas Jefferson, 14 March 1801, in Cappon, ed., *The Adams–Jefferson Letters*, p. 264.

18 Quoted in McCullough, *John Adams*, p. 572.

19 Letter from John Adams to Benjamin Rush, 6 February 1805, in Butterfield, ed., *Letters of Benjamin Rush*. "Surgeon" and "lieutenant" refer to two of Rush's sons.

20 Letter from Benjamin Rush to John Adams, 19 February 1805, in Butterfield, ed., *Letters of Benjamin Rush*, p. 890.

21 McCullough, *The Course of Human Events*, Jefferson Lecture in the Humanities.

22 Dreams recorded by wounded patriots are difficult to find; those that survive are contained in their diaries and letters.

23 In a letter from Rush to Adams, dated 19 February 1805, Rush said Adams was like Sancho in *Don Quixote* who, when asked how he liked his government, responded not to the question, but to his immediate and pressing interest, his cold feet, and asked for his socks.

24 Letter from Adams to Rush, 27 February 1805, in Butterfield, ed., *Letters of Benjamin Rush*.

25 Letter from Rush to Adams, 23 March 1805 in Butterfield, ed., *Letters of Benjamin Rush*. Rush quotes Horace, Satires. I.i. 69–70.

26 Ibid.

27 Letter from Adams to Rush, 11 April 1805, in Butterfield, ed., *Letters of Benjamin Rush*.

28 The poem is "Hans Carvel" (1701, lines 89–94) by Matthew Prior. Quoted in Butterfield, ed., *Letters of Benjamin Rush*.

29 See M.-L. von Franz, *Dreams: A Study of the Dreams of Jung, Descartes, Socrates, and Other Historical Figures* (Boston: Shambhala, 1998).

30 Ibid., p. 1.

31 The trident was adopted in its positive aspect as the caduceus staff and is usually feathered with a serpent as part of Mercury's accoutrement. It is also an emblem of the American Medical Association. Rush's image is an emblem of the American

Psychiatric Association. The trident is the symbol for the word *psychology*.

32 C.G. Jung, "The Philosophical Tree" (1954), in *CW*, vol. 13 (Princeton, N.J.: Princeton University Press, 1967), par. 450.

33 Von Franz, *Dreams*, p. 130.

34 Ibid.

35 Letter from Adams to Rush, 29 November 1812, in Butterfield, ed., *Letters of Benjamin Rush.*

36 Ibid.

37 Letter from Rush to Adams, 14 December 1812, in Butterfield, ed., *Letters of Benjamin Rush.*

38 Letter from John Adams to Abigail Adams, in McCullough, *1776*, p. 447.

39 Letter from Abigail Adams to Mary Cranch, 30 May 1790, ibid., p. 423.

40 McCullough, *John Adams*, p. 423.

41 *Animalus* is related to animus ("spirit") and is the root of the word and the symbolic idea *animal.* The term *annimatical* is found in Renaissance astrology, used by Heinrich Cornelius Agrippa in his theories on magic.

42 Louise Robbins, *Elephant Slaves and Pampered Parrots: Exotic Animals in Eighteenth-century Paris* (Baltimore: Johns Hopkins University Press, 2002), p. 21.

43 Ibid.

44 Letter from Adams to Rush, 29 November 1812, in Butterfield, ed., *Letters of Benjamin Rush.*

45 Edward F. Edinger, *Anatomy of the Psyche: Alchemical Symbolism in Psychotherapy* (LaSalle, Ill.: Open Court Publishing Company, 1985), p. 198.

46 Edward F. Edinger, *The Bible and the Psyche: Individuation Symbolism in the Old Testament* (Toronto: Inner City Books, 1986), pp. 22–23.

47 Letter from Adams to Rush, 12 September 1811, in Butterfield, ed., *Letters of Benjamin Rush.*

48 Letter from Adams to Rush, 11 November 1807, in Butterfield, ed., *Letters of Benjamin Rush.*

49 Butterfield, ed., *Letters of Benjamin Rush*, p. 242.

50 Schutz and Adair, eds., *The Spur of Fame*, p. 13.

51 Author's note: I discovered this poem, written in Rush's own hand on a single sheet of paper, at the Rosenbach Museum and Library. Undated and not yet transcribed, it was included with his assorted Revolutionary War papers. It is analyzed here as Rush's composition, however, a very similar poem with this title has also been attributed to Annis Stockton (1783–1891) [Carla Mulford, editor, *Only for the Eye of a Friend: The Poems of Annis Boudinot Stockton* (Charlottesville: University Press of Virginia, 1995), p. 233].

52 Letter from Rush to Adams, 21 August 1812, in Butterfield, ed., *Letters of Benjamin Rush.* See also John Adams's dream of 1812 (p. 75), in which he took up the theme of party divisions.

53 Letter from Rush to Adams, 26 December 1811, in Schutz and Adair, eds., *The Spur of Fame*, p. 220.

54 Schutz and Adair, eds., *The Spur of Fame*, p. 139, n5.

55 Letter from Rush to Adams, 16 September 1808, in Butterfield, ed., *Letters of Benjamin Rush*.

56 Ibid.

57 Letter from Rush to Adams, 16 September 1808, in Schutz and Adair, eds., *The Spur of Fame*, p. 129.

58 Letter from Adams to Rush, 27 September 1808, in Schutz and Adair, eds., *The Spur of Fame*, p. 131.

59 C.G. Jung, *Memories, Dreams, Reflections* (New York: Vintage, 1989), p. 237.

60 Letter from Abigail Adams to Thomas Jefferson, 25 October 1804, in Cappon, ed., *The Adams-Jefferson Letters*, pp. 280–81.

61 Letter from Rush to Adams, 21 November 1805, in Butterfield, ed., *Letters of Benjamin Rush*.

62 Letter from Rush to Adams, 10 June 1806, in Butterfield, ed., *Letters of Benjamin Rush*.

63 That is, symbolic of the eternal sacred marriage with the future. Abigail Adams's story lives on in archetypal form and has the potential to influence our own lives.

64 McCullough, *The Course of Human Events*, Jefferson Lecture in the Humanities.

65 Letter from Abigail Adams to Thomas Jefferson, 20 May 1804, in Schutz and Adair, eds., *The Spur of Fame*, pp. 265–266.

66 L. H. Butterfield, "The Dream of Benjamin Rush: The Reconciliation of John Adams and Thomas Jefferson," *Yale Review* 40, p. 300.

67 Letter from Jefferson to Abigail Adams, 13 June 1804, in Cappon, ed., *The Adams-Jefferson Letters*, p. 269.

68 Letter from Abigail Adams to Jefferson, 20 May 1804, in Cappon, ed., *The Adams-Jefferson Letters*, p. 268.

69 Letter from Adams to Rush, 4 March 1809, in Butterfield, "The Dream of Benjamin Rush," p. 299.

70 Letter from Rush to Adams, 16 October 1809, in Butterfield, "The Dream of Benjamin Rush," p. 301.

71 Ibid.

72 Benjamin Rush, *Medical Inquiries and Observations upon the Diseases of the Mind* (New York: Hafner, 1962), p. 271.

73 Von Franz, *Dreams*, p. 27.

74 Letter from Rush to Adams, 2 January 1811, in Butterfield, ed., *Letters of Benjamin Rush*.

75 Letter from Rush to Adams, 20 August 1811, in Butterfield, ed., *Letters of Benjamin Rush*.

76 Ibid.

77 Letter from Adams to Rush, 28 August 1811, in Schutz and Adair, eds., *The Spur of Fame*, p. 207.

78 Letter from Rush to Adams, 4 September 1811, in Butterfield, ed., *Letters of Benjamin Rush*.

79 Letter from Rush to Adams, 16 December 1811, in Butterfield, ed., *Letters of Benjamin Rush*.

80 Letter from Adams to Rush, 25 December 1811, in Schutz and Adair, eds., *The Spur of Fame*, p. 220.

81 Letter from Rush to Adams, 14 December 1812, in Schutz and Adair, eds., *The Spur of Fame*, p. 282.

82 Ibid. Mr. Clymer, a signer of the Declaration of Independence, was the first Treasurer of the United States.

83 Jacob Jones, commander of the *Wasp*, captured the British ship *Frolic*. Schutz and Adair, eds., *The Spur of Fame*, p. 283, n15.

84 Sarah Siddons (1755–1831) was a well-known actress of the London stage.

85 This line does not appear to be a legitimate biblical reference. It may be a dream invention.

86 A dream of John Adams, 8 December 1812, as excerpted in Schutz and Adair, eds., *The Spur of Fame*, p. 283.

87 Adam, from "adamah," meaning earth, is a union of the opposites, spirit and earth. Eve, from "em" is a root for "mother of all." The word *eve* indicates the time just prior to an event and portends a division of the union of opposites.

88 Letter from Adams to Rush, 8 December 1812, in Schutz and Adair, eds., *The Spur of Fame*, p. 283.

89 Rush to Adams, 8 January 1813, in Schutz and Adair, eds., *The Spur of Fame*, p. 294.

90 Adams to Rush, 15 January 1813, in Schutz and Adair, eds., *The Spur of Fame*, p. 296.

91 Enclosure in a letter from Rush to Adams, 19 December 1812, in Schutz and Adair, eds., *The Spur of Fame*, p. 295.

92 Letter from Adams to Rush, 4 January 1813, in Schutz and Adair, eds., *The Spur of Fame*, p. 296.

93 Schutz and Adair, eds., *The Spur of Fame*, p. 284.

94 Ibid., p. 287.

95 Ibid.

96 C. G. Jung, "Synchronicity: An Acausal Connecting Principle" (1952), in *CW*, vol. 8 (Princeton, N.J.: Princeton University Press, 1969), par. 870.

97 Schutz and Adair, eds., *The Spur of Fame*, p. 287.

98 Quoted by Rush in a letter to Adams, 16 December 1811, in Schutz and Adair, eds., *The Spur of Fame*, p. 216.

99 Letter from Jefferson to Adams, 21 January 1812, in Cappon, ed., *The Adams-Jefferson Letters*.

100 Letter from Adams to Jefferson, 20 October 1818, in Cappon, ed., *The Adams-Jefferson Letters*.

101 Letter from Rush to Adams, 10 April 1813, in Schutz and Adair, eds., *The Spur of Fame*, p. 305. This was written just eight days before Rush's death.

102 Letter from Adams to Rush, 18 April 1813, in Schutz and Adair, eds., *The Spur of Fame*, p. 306. The

quotation is from Alexander Pope, "An Essay on Man," Epistle 6.388.

103   Letter from Adams to Julia Rush, 24 April 1813, in Butterfield, ed., *Letters of Benjamin Rush.*

104   Letter from Jefferson to Adams, 27 May 1813, in Cappon, ed., *The Adams-Jefferson Letters.*

105   Letter from Adams to Jefferson, 11 June 1813, in Cappon, ed., *The Adams-Jefferson Letters.*

106   Letter from Rush to Adams, 4 July 1810, in Cappon, ed., *The Adams-Jefferson Letters*, p. 179.

107   C.G. Jung, quoted in Sara Corbett, "The Holy Grail of the Unconscious," *New York Times* magazine, September 20, 2009.

bibliography

Adams, Henry. *The Education of Henry Adams.* New York: The Modern
Library, 1931.

Adams, John. 1797 Inaugural Speech. In David McCullough, *John Adams.*
New York: Simon and Schuster, 2002, p. 567.

Brookhiser, Richard. *America's First Dynasty: The Adamses 1735–1918.* New York:
The Free Press, 2002.

Bullock, Steven C. *Revolutionary Brotherhood: Freemasonry and the Transformation
of the American Social Order, 1730–1840.* Chapel Hill: The University of North
Carolina Press, 1996.

Butterfield, L.H. "The Dream of Benjamin Rush: The Reconciliation of John
Adams and Thomas Jefferson." *Yale Review* 40 (Winter): 297–319.

Butterfield, L. H., editor. *Letters of Benjamin Rush,* 2 vols. Princeton, N.J.: Princeton
University Press, 1951.

———. *The Adams Papers: Diary and Autobiography of John Adams,* 4 vols.
Cambridge, Mass.: Belknap Press of Harvard University Press, 1962.

Cappon, Lester J., editor. *The Adams-Jefferson Letters: The Complete Correspondence
Between Thomas Jefferson and Abigail and John Adams.* Chapel Hill:
The University of North Carolina Press, 1988.

Corbett, Sara. "The Holy Grail of the Unconscious," *New York Times* magazine,
September 20, 2009.

Durant, Will. *The Story of Philosophy: The Lives and Opinions of the World's Greatest
Philosophers from Plato to John Dewey.* New York: Simon and Schuster, 1961.

Durant, Will and Ariel. *The Story of Civilization.* Vol. ii, *The Age of Napoleon.*
New York: MJF Books, 1997.

Diggins, John Patrick. *John Adams.* New York: Times Books, 2003.

Edinger, Edward F. *Anatomy of the Psyche: Alchemical Symbolism in Psychotherapy.*
LaSalle, Ill.: Open Court Publishing Company, 1985.

———. *The Bible and the Psyche: Individuation Symbolism in the Old Testament.*
Toronto: Inner City Books, 1986.

———. *The Mystery of the Coniunctio: Alchemical Image of Individuation.* Toronto:
Inner City Books, 1994.

Elkins, Stanley, and Eric McKitrick. *The Age of Federalism: The Early American
Republic, 1788–1800.* New York: Oxford University Press, 1995.

Ellis, Joseph J. *Founding Brothers: The Revolutionary Generation.* New York:
Knopf, 2000.

———. *Passionate Sage: The Character and Legacy of John Adams.* New York:
W. W. Norton, 2001.

Graves, Robert. Introduction to *New Larousse Encyclopedia of Mythology.* London:
The Hamlyn Publishing Group, 1959.

Henderson, J. L. "C. G. Jung's Psychology: Additions and Extensions." *Journal of Analytical Psychology* 36 (1991):429–42.

Jung, C. G. *Memories, Dreams, Reflections.* New York: Vintage, 1989.

———. "On the Nature of the Psyche" (1954), in *CW,* vol. 8. Princeton, N.J.: Princeton University Press, 1969.

———. "The Philosophical Tree" (1954), in *CW,* vol. 13. Princeton, N.J.: Princeton University Press, 1967.

———. "Synchronicity: An Acausal Connecting Principle" (1952), in *CW,* vol. 8. Princeton, N.J.: Princeton University Press, 1969.

McCullough, David. *1776.* New York: Simon and Schuster, 2006.

———. *John Adams.* New York: Simon and Schuster, 2002.

———. *The Course of Human Events.* Jefferson Lecture in the Humanities, Washington, D.C., 2005. Audioworks, 2003. Compact disk.

Morgan, Speer, and Greg Michalson, editors. *For Our Beloved Country: American War Diaries from the Revolution to the Persian Gulf.* New York: Atlantic Monthly Press, 1994.

Morison, Samuel Eliot. *The Oxford History of American People.* New York: Oxford University Press, 1965.

Morison, Samuel Eliot, Henry Steele Commager, and William E. Leuchtenburg. *The Growth of the American Republic,* vol. 1, rev. ed. New York: Oxford University Press, 1955.

Morris, Richard B. *Witnesses at the Creation: Hamilton, Madison, Jay, and the Constitution.* New York: Barnes and Noble, 1996.

Mulford, Carla, editor. *Only for the Eye of a Friend: The Poems of Annis Boudinot Stockton.* Charlottesville: University Press of Virginia, 1995.

Progoff, Ira. *Jung, Synchronicity, and Human Destiny: Noncausal Dimensions of Human Experience.* New York: Dell, 1973.

Robbins, Louise. *Elephant Slaves and Pampered Parrots: Exotic Animals in Eighteenth-century Paris.* Baltimore: Johns Hopkins University Press, 2002.

Rush, Benjamin. *Essays, Literary, Moral, and Philosophical.* Philadelphia: Thomas and Samuel F. Bradford, 1806.

———. *Medical Inquiries and Observations upon the Diseases of the Mind.* New York: Hafner, 1962.

———. *Two Essays on the Mind.* New York: Brunner/Mazel, 1972.

Schutz, John A., and Douglass Adair, eds. *The Spur of Fame.* Indianapolis: The Liberty Fund, 2001.

Stein, Murray, ed. *Jungian Analysis.* LaSalle, Ill.: Open Court, 1982.

von Franz, M.-L. *Dreams: A Study of the Dreams of Jung, Descartes, Socrates, and Other Historical Figures.* Boston: Shambhala, 1998.

———. *Individuation in Fairy Tales.* Boston: Shambhala, 1977.

Weymouth, L., ed. *Thomas Jefferson: The Man, His World, His Influence.* New York: G. P. Putnam's Sons, 1974.

Whyte, Lancelot Law. *The Unconscious Before Freud.* Garden City, N.Y.: Anchor Doubleday, 1962.

a c k n o w l e d g m e n t s

A heartfelt thank you in memory of Dr. Joseph Henderson, Jungian analyst and mentor to me, who encouraged me to write this book long ago. Particular and affectionate thanks to Margaret Ryan for her encouragement, support, and editorial guidance. Grateful appreciation to Siobhan Drummond, Murray Stein, and Chiron Publications for polishing and publishing this book. Thanks also to the research departments at UCLA, Princeton University, the *Yale Review* staff, and the University of Pennsylvania for their assistance. I extend appreciation to the Massachusetts and Philadelphia Historical Societies for providing access to the Adams and Rush collections. Special thanks to Nicholas Noyes of the Maine Historical Society for organizing a research team to help me read and screen diaries and letters of Revolutionary War soldiers looking for notations of their dreams. Thank you to the Rosenbach Museum and Library in Philadelphia for granting access to Dr. Rush's unpublished poem and papers. A highlight of the research process was the gracious assistance of the Pennsylvania Hospital which allowed me access to Benjamin Rush's original operating room, records, and models in the Old Hospital. Thank you to my efficient bibliographer Jonah Elliot Zarrow, and to his able associate Jennifer Leigh Erickson. Most special thanks to ZFD for their patience and affection during this long process. And finally, grateful thanks to Stanton Zarrow, my lifelong friend, for his unwavering support and (often inexplicable) confidence in me.

SHEILA DICKMAN ZARROW, PH.D.

CALIFORNIA 2010

index

Note: italic page number indicates an illustration.

active imagination, 58

Adams, Abigail, 1–2, 9, 15–16, 19–21, 46, 66–67, 92, 103n12; correspondence with Thomas Jefferson, 63, 66–68

Adams, Charles, 2, 9, 19

Adams, John, *6* (*see also* color gallery), 26; America's first vice president, 45; annimatical dream, 44, 47–50, 60, 81, 88, 90; autobiography, 8–9, 99; bid for reelection, x, 1, 5–6, 12; death, 71, 94; desire for public recognition, 51; family, 18–19; as a farmer, 19, 51; financial concerns, 19; health, 8; leaving the White House, 5–7; personal style, 17; popularity, ix; publishing as an outlet, 21; relationship with Benjamin Rush, 5, 27, 55–56; relationship with Thomas Jefferson, 20, 65–66, 69–73, 91–94, 99; signer of the Declaration of Independence, 3; statue in Worcester, Massachusetts, x–xi, 97; as a symbol, xi; theater dream, 50, 79–85, 87–88, 90, 92 (*see also* dreams, of John Adams)

Adams, John Quincy, 2, 7, 16, 19, 21, 63, 99

Adams, Louisa Catherine, 2

Adams, Thomas, 19

Adamses, home in Braintree, Massachusetts, 2, 16–17

Agrippa, Heinrich Cornelius, 105n41

alchemy, 49

alcohol, 60–62, 65

Alien and Sedition Acts, 61

alterity principle, 3

American economy, in the early years of the Republic, 46–47

American Revolution, 47, 49, 99; writing the history, 21 (*see also* Revolutionary War)

analytical psychology, 41

anima, 54, 82–86

animals, as symbols, 88

animus, xii

archetype: of rebirth, 25; of the physician/healer, 42; of theater, 79–81; numbers as, 90

Asclepiadae, 37

Asclepius, 37

Bill of Rights, 47

Bonaparte, Napoleon, 10

Boreas, 18, 35

Boston Tea Party, 3–4, 82

Briesler, John, 1–2

Butterfield, L.H., 103n5

Cabot, Edward Clark, 103n4

caduceus, 37

Chiron, 88, *89*

Christ, 34–35

Christ Church, 26, 29–30, 34–35

Christian religion, 44 (*see also* religion)

church, and state, 26, 33

Civil War, 47

Clymer, George, 106n82

Constitution, of the United States, 4, 47, 68

Continental Army, 26, 53

Darwin, Charles, 59

Darwin, Erasmus, 59

Declaration of Independence, 1, 3–4, 25, 94
democracy, 3, 9, 31, 68
Descartes, René, 33, 39–40, 85
devil. *See* Satan
dreams and dreaming, x, 9, 31–32, 35–37, 45, 48, 57–58, 60, 90; archetypal, 45; of Benjamin Rush, xi–xii, 95; of Continental Army soldiers, 26; of John Adams, xi–xii, 79, 95; of the author, xi–xii, 95; prophetic, 72; writing of, 32, 57
dyspraxia, 96

Embargo Act of 1807, 59, 61
Eros, 82–84
Eve, 84–86

faith, 40, 52
feminine, 60, 84–85
Franklin, Benjamin, 24, 30, 45
French Revolution, 46, 70
Frolic, H.B.M. Sloop of War, *78* (*see also* color gallery)

Galen of Pergamum, 42
Gerry, Elbridge, 10–11
God ideal, 40
golden mean, 49

Hamilton, Alexander, 47
Hamilton, Edith, ix
Hermes, *38,* 39
Hippocrates, 37, 41
History of Medicine (mosaic), *41* (*see also* color gallery)
Hobby (Adams's horse), 75, 87–90
Horace, 104n25
Hull, Isaac, *76,* 84

Imhotep, 42
individuation, 39, 86, 88
Isis, 42

Jefferson, Thomas, 6–7, 18, 20, 26, 28, 30, 46, 50, 68, *93* (*see also* color gallery); as vice president, 6, 11–12; correspondence with Abigail Adams, 63, 66–68; correspondence with Benjamin Rush, 14, 58, 63; death, 71, 94; family, 66–67; home at Monticello, 17; inauguration, 9, 13; intellectual peer of Benjamin Rush, 59, 63–64; relationship with John Adams, 20, 65–66, 69–73, 91–94, 99
Jones, Jacob, *76,* 84
Jung, Carl Gustav, ix, 31, 41, 58, 62, 72, 97; Red Book, 95

Kant, Immanuel, 33
King George III, 3
King Louis XVI, 48, 81
Knox, Henry, 4

Madison, James, 14, 46, 69
madness. *See* mental illness
mandala, 33, 40, 85
McCullough, David, ix
menagerie, as a symbol, 48–49
mental illness, 26, 31–33
Mercury, 29, 31, 33–39, *34, 38,* 41
monuments, to founding fathers, 18, 53
mythic figures, 37–39

nationhood, 79
Native Americans, relations with settlers, 24–25
navy, of the newly formed United States, 4–5, 46, 82
Neptune, 34–35

opposites, united, 47, 49, 54, 60, 81, 85, 107n87

peace treaty, with France (1799), 10–12
Peacefield, 103n13 (*see also* Stoneyfield)
play, within a dream, 79, 92
political parties, division between, 56, 65

Pope, Alexander, 107n102
Poseidon. *See* Neptune
psyche, x; and soma, 26; as a stage, 81–82;
    collective, of America, 3; religious
    function of, 41
psychology, ix, 33, 103n5, 104n31

religion, 40; and philosophy, 32; role
    in the new government, 31
    (*see also* church, and state)
Revolutionary War, 3, 39, 53, 68
Rush, Benjamin, xi, *6* (*see also* color
    gallery), 13; as a physician-healer,
    27, 37, 46; as politician, 27, 39;
    background, 24–25; connection to
    Christianity, 30; correspondence
    with Thomas Jefferson, 14, 58, 63;
    dreams, 26–31, 33–42, 45, 59–62, 69;
    prophetic dream, 71, 92, 94; study
    of dreams, 40, 71; intellectual peer
    of Thomas Jefferson, 59, 63–64;
    intuition, 55, 64–65; approach to
    mental illness, 31–3; job at the Mint,
    14; physician general, 26, 52; poetry,
    57–58; focus on psychiatry, 37–40;
    desire for public recognition, 51;
    publishing, 103n11; relationship
    with John Adams, 5, 27, 55–56;
    role in history, 99; signer of the
    Declaration of Independence, 3, 25
Rush, Julia, 94

Satan, 34–35, 40
scaffold, as a symbol, 49
Sedgwick, Theodore, 9–11
Self, 33, 41, 48, 58, 80, 82, 88
self-knowledge, 32–33
shadow, 40
Shakespeare, William, 84
Shaw, Billy, 1–2
Siddons, Sarah, 77, *80*, 82–85, *83*
    (*see also* color gallery)

slavery, 47
soma. *See* psyche, and soma
soul, 54, 95–97; disorder of, 31–32
stage, as a symbol. *See* theater,
    as a symbol
Stockton, Annis, 105n51
Stoneyfield, 16
symbol, 34–35 (*see also* animals,
    wind, trident, menagerie,
    scaffold, theater)
synchronicity, 37, 45, 52, 72, 79, 87

Tallyrand, 10
theater, as a symbol, 81–85
trident, as a symbol, 29, 33–37, 104n31
typology, Rush's, 64

unconscious, 31, 34–35, 45, 48, 58, 62, 88,
    99; collective, 82

Versailles, 43–44, 48, 75, 79, 81
Vesalius, 42
vice president, of the United States, 6
von Franz, Marie-Louise, 72, 82–84

War of 1812, 50
Washington, George, 5–6, 18, 21, 26,
    30, 46, 52, 53, 66–68; as General
    of the Armies, 25; home at Mount
    Vernon, 17
Wasp, U.S. Sloop of War, *78*
    (*see also* color gallery)
White House, 1–2, 5, 7, 9
wind, as a symbol, 29–30, 33, 35, 39–40
writing, 58

XYZ affair, 10

yellow fever, 13, 26, 46

www.ingramcontent.com/pod-product-compliance
Lightning Source LLC
Chambersburg PA
CBHW050233270326
41914CB00033BB/1902/J